TACKLING MISCONCEPTIC
IN PRIMARY MATHEMATICS

Did you know that a circle has more than one side? Are you aware of the difference between 1:2 and ½? Could you spot when a 2-D shape is actually 3-D?

Tackling Misconceptions in Primary Mathematics is a practical guide based on the principles that sound subject knowledge is key to fostering understanding, and addressing misconceptions is central to pupil progress. With an emphasis on preventing as well as unpicking misconceptions in the classroom, it offers trainee and practising teachers clear explanations, practical strategies, and examples of the classroom language and dialogue that will help pupils successfully navigate tricky topics.

The book demonstrates the importance of preventing misconceptions through what is said, done and presented to children, giving a variety of examples of common misconceptions and exploring how they can be addressed in a classroom environment. Proper intervention at the point of misconception is regarded as a key skill for any outstanding classroom practitioner and Kieran Mackle stresses the value in understanding how the pupil got there and explaining that it's okay to make mistakes. Misconceptions are only one step away from correctly formed concepts if harnessed with care and skill.

This comprehensive text is designed to be read as either a short course introduction, or dipped into as a guide to assist teaching. It is essential reading for trainee primary school teachers on all routes to QTS, as well as mathematics subject leaders and practising teachers looking to inspire the next generation of confident and inquisitive mathematicians.

Kieran Mackle is a MaST (Primary Mathematics Specialist Teacher), action researcher and a Specialist Leader of Education, who has worked with numerous schools and the Medway local authority to provide training and school-to-school support. He is Mathematics Subject Leader, Year 6 teacher and Deputy Head at St. Michael's Primary School, Chatham, UK.

TACKLING MISCONCEPTIONS IN PRIMARY MATHEMATICS

Preventing, identifying and addressing children's errors

Kieran Mackle

Routledge
Taylor & Francis Group

LONDON AND NEW YORK

First published 2017
by Routledge
2 Park Square, Milton Park, Abingdon, Oxon OX14 4RN

and by Routledge
711 Third Avenue, New York, NY 10017

Routledge is an imprint of the Taylor & Francis Group, an informa business

British Library Cataloguing in Publication Data
A catalogue record for this book is available from the British Library

Library of Congress Cataloging in Publication Data
Names: Mackle, Kieran.
Title: Tackling misconceptions in primary mathematics : preventing, identifying and addressing children's errors / Kieran Mackle.
Description: New York : Routledge, 2017. | Includes bibliographical references.
Identifiers: LCCN 2016013502 | ISBN 9781138903784 (hardback) | ISBN 9781138906303 (pbk.) | ISBN 9781315695570 (ebook)
Subjects: LCSH: Mathematics--Study and teaching--United States.
Classification: LCC QA13 .M133 2017 | DDC 372.7--dc23
LC record available at http://lccn.loc.gov/2016013502

ISBN: 978-1-138-90378-4 (hbk)
ISBN: 978-1-138-90630-3 (pbk)
ISBN: 978-1-315-69557-0 (ebk)

Typeset in Interstate
by Saxon Graphics Ltd, Derby

Many thanks must go to the family members and colleagues who have continually inspired and sustained the creation of this book with their unconditional support and guidance, for without their intellectual and emotional sustenance it would not have been possible.

CONTENTS

CONTENTS

PROLOGUE

When the notion of writing a book about misconceptions in mathematics came into my head I was heavily involved in professional development which guided me quite naturally it seems in the direction of the work of Julie Ryan, Julian Williams, Derek Haylock, Ian Thompson and Candia Morgan, to name but a few of the leading experts in education research. Their work, and the work of many others, has had a profound impact on my classroom practice and I can attest, anecdotally of course, to the bearing a reasonable familiarisation with education research can have on one's own practice.

In January 2014 I was lucky enough to take part in a research project organised by the National College for Teaching and Leadership which involved the analysis of education systems and practices on a global scale. The aim of this ambitious project was to take 50 Specialist Leaders of Education (SLEs in shorthand) nearly half way across the world, to Shanghai and Ningbo to be precise, in search of practices that could effectively transfer into our classrooms and schools with the overall aim of enhancing the quality of mathematics education on offer to pupils in England. The range of SLEs was expansive both geographically and, most importantly, in terms of the ages and backgrounds of the pupil cohorts represented. In terms of my own professional development this was a fantastic experience and participation allowed me to develop my ever evolving view of the world of mathematics education.

There are many talking points surrounding the nature of such research alone; we must always consider the effectiveness of the OECD/PISA testing as a marker of effective teaching, many important cultural differences exist between China and England, not least the expectations of what school should actually look like, and the working lives of teachers in their respective time zones. In addition to this only three subjects, Chinese, Maths and English, are taught in Shanghai schools and teachers only spend an average of 30% of their school day involved in what their English counterparts have come to know as 'contact time' or, more explicitly, time with a whole class of pupils. The rest of their time is spent running small group or 1:1 sessions during which they fill gaps or intervene where pupils have developed misconceptions, or they are conducting action research with their peers.

I'll stop short of adding a photograph to what may seem an advertisement for teaching in China because teachers in Shanghai, at the time of my visit certainly, expected to earn no more than the equivalent of £10,000 a year, less than half of what a newly qualified teacher in England can expect as an entrance salary. So while they enjoy much greater freedom in their working day and what appears to be a more manageable work/life balance, they must supplement their earnings through private tuition and other endeavours. Swings and roundabouts of the highest order.

This may appear a tangent but really the preceding two paragraphs serve to provide context for the nugget of gold I brought back from China. A research based approach to classroom practice not only serves to enhance the knowledge and understanding of the practitioners involved but for the pupils in their care as well. I have tried at least two models since returning from China and have not yet found the right balance but you can be sure that when I do, you'll be reading about that too. The main success, and I was already much of the way there, is in my own professional development for since returning I have redoubled my efforts to seek out the best and most relevant sources of research applicable to primary education. For as I improve, so too do the opportunities I provide for my pupils. If China taught me anything then it was to continually improve myself while trying to improve others.

The 'Lesson Study' approach to professional development is one that sits well with my cognitive biases as I firmly believe seeing teaching and learning in action is the best way to develop a greater understanding of our own practice. This particular approach, without delving into too technical a description, requires groups of teachers to plan, deliver and reflect on a series of lessons together. The groups often plan together and take turns delivering the actual lessons. Then they come together to reflect on the successes and areas for improvement before planning a new lesson based on the ascertained information and repeating the sequence ad infinitum. Naturally some sort of measure of the development of the teachers involved will be instated, presumably but not always necessarily, by some echelon of the school's leadership so the time on offer to work with a given group of your peers may not always be as infinite in nature as I have portrayed but you get the gist of what I'm saying.

I have found that this model can be adapted to suit the needs to fewer teachers and that effective coaching methods can be employed alongside team teaching, whereby the planning and reflection are still done collaboratively, but really you need to find the system which is best for you. Combine this or a similar approach with the most up to date research and you may find the winning combination for your own professional development. More important, he says in an altruistic manner which is both genuine and sincere, it is a win-win situation for the pupils in your care as well.

As the proposal became a reality and I was asked to consider my 'competitors' I was quite disconcerted with the idea that I was 'competing' with anyone in the world of education, principally because when all is said and done there is but one thing we have in mind, the education of the children in our care and the fostering of positive attitudes towards mathematics, clinical fluency in execution of mathematical skills and an overall/general preparation for the world of the future that they will one day come to inhabit. Well, they are my guiding principles at least and I find it difficult to imagine why anyone would join the profession if these ideas did not feature quite prominently on their list of reasons for waking up every Monday morning. Perhaps even Tuesday and Wednesday morning for that matter as well.

My point, however, is that it is not for me to say what you should read and when you should read it. There is a wealth of mathematical research available and one piece has the ability to take you in an entirely different direction to which you imagined you would travel as your interest is captured and the relevance to your daily practice creates meaningful and relevant links to your world and the window through which you perceive it. A balance,

I find, must be struck between the theoretical and practical in which the two are married to create the optimum conditions for outstanding practice to take place which will, in turn, lead to true and meaningful progress being made by the pupils in your care, whether that be in a classroom of 20, a school of 400 or a local authority of thousands.

It is my intention that this book draws on my experience and learning to provide you with an understanding of the strategies I have found to work and the endless possibilities on offer to all in the teaching profession. When bouncing the idea for this book from colleague to colleague I was concerned with the misconceptions we hold as teachers which don't fit the reality of the mathematical world we live in and worried about how it could be possible to exist in a time or culture where it is sometimes acceptable to admit to being 'bad at mathematics'. And while it may form the centrepiece of further discussions other than this I must admit I am perplexed and that it can be tolerable to admit what is tantamount to innumeracy while simultaneously no one would dare cry illiteracy, certainly not in the nonchalant manner I have found anyway.

Little did I know, however, that reform of the National Curriculum in England, on which consultation took place in circa June 2012 and which eventually manifested itself as the 2014 National Curriculum, would place such emphasis on the priorities I held so dear; the explicit use of language, mathematical accuracy and relevance to real life but a few examples. Though when I think about it, it was highly unlikely I was the only one to draw the conclusions I had drawn and greater men than me must have considered the impact these principles and approaches could have to the standards of mathematics on a national level.

Yet the best thing for me is how the key themes of this book and that of the National Curriculum have the power to transcend both time and space. This is no hyperbolic assertion on my part, of which I am fully aware I am capable of, rather it is a testament to the power of mathematics in its purest form. For what really is it to use mathematically accurate language, what is it to insist that every child is fluent and what is it to insist that mathematics has a relevance that will no doubt foster a love of the subject and eventually allow those same pupils to be the abstract mathematicians of the future.

We are in a prime position to have a much greater impact than we ever imagined and I fully believe whether you practise your craft in Abu Dhabi, Zagreb or anywhere in between, the principles can remain the same. The power is in your hands. With one, take a hold of any research you can, with the other take a hold of your practice and strive for perfection, although elusive by its very definition, and always, always aim to provide the best education for those in your care.

From this I hope you can garner that I have no prior or current relationship with any of the products, companies or organisations I recommend practitioners use in the pages of this book. As should be clear from the delivery of the information my own experience and reading form the basis of the guidance given. I do this merely for the love of mathematics and a deep vocational desire to help provide an outstanding education for as many pupils as possible.

Pre-emptive explanation

At a slight tangent perhaps, the term facilitator of learning is reasonably commonplace at present and I believe may have been coined by the research of Knowles (1975), in relation to self-directed adult education. And while I believe that facilitation forms much of the role we have to play in and out of the classroom I accept that it is not necessarily accepted as a universal truth and you must reconcile your understanding of your role with my generalisations and advice. It is an example, you might say, of the idiosyncratic controversies littered throughout education which I believe ensure practitioners, largely of the informed and proactive kind, will continually try to maintain their commitment to professional/self-development and education in an increasingly changing landscape. While the tenuous nature of this paragraph is clear for all to see it is not my desire to justify every comment or pedagogical assertion with every other possible counter-argument but rather to make it clear early on that there are many schools of thought and many conversations taking place as we speak.

The use of social media by the education world is astounding and very much for the betterment of our professional development and voice. It does, however, make me quite wary of the fact that there is always someone with an equally vehement belief in approaches contrary to your own. Be aware that there are many ways to skin a cat and, if Greek tragedies have taught us nothing else, pride always comes before the fall. If you are aiming to achieve a state in which everything is sussed and a final level of excellence has been reached then you are in the wrong profession. You may develop proficiency but there is always something else to learn. Take as much as you can on board, develop your style and run with it. That is the best we can hope for but remember you will never waste your time looking at the clock and wishing for home time. I can guarantee such an occurrence is highly improbable.

Reference

Knowles, M. (1975) *Self-Directed Learning*. Chicago: Follet.

INTRODUCTION

At one, perhaps all too recent, point in time it was said the government could track a child from the age of 5 to 16 and exponentially predict the progress they should make if certain markers were met at given points in their education careers. A child with a good level of development, or GLD as it is commonly recognised, on entry to Year 1 had a better than average chance of attaining Level 2b at the end of Key Stage 1. A child attaining Level 2b was thus expected to easily reach Level 4 by the end of Key Stage 2, which in itself was an indicator of the likelihood a child would attain a C grade at GCSE. Gone are any preconceived notions of free will and volition. On the contrary, it appears an education can be so finitely mapped out that it may even be possible to forget that children are indeed children and unique and wired to reject conformity by their very nature. Of course, the National Curriculum Levels, as outlined in the late 1990s revision of the only statutory document in English education, are no longer in use. So we cannot currently, with any great certainty or conviction, say what level is paramount to the attainment of subsequent levels. However, once the limbo we currently find ourselves in comes to an end it will be possible, I expect, to track children from their entry point in Nursery, 3 years old and but a babe in arms, to Key Stage 1, Key Stage 2 and eventually GCSE grade C, 1-9, or IB if the case may be, and beyond.

The measure, I believe, is irrelevant but the importance of the impact you can have on the mathematical future of the children in your care should be clear for all to see. The mathematicians inside us all will naturally want our pupils to be in the midst of the select group who continue on to graduate level and strive for the answers hidden somewhere in the collective language of the universe (mathematics) and it should be our intention to inspire generations of mathematicians to come. However, where this is not possible we must strive to ensure the highest quality understanding so that it may be applied in the fields they eventually do end up in.

The responsibility comes with great reward as you already know, or will soon find out, but it must be infinitely clear that the responsibility is yours. By opening this book you have taken the first step to ensure the children in your care receive the high quality provision they deserve. Mathematics is a universal language which helps us to make sense of the world we live in. The Chinese, for example, are a people who have chosen not to adopt a standardised alphabet yet see the benefit in the use of the Arabic number system. The world our children are set to grow up in has not yet been created, the careers they will choose not yet invented. If Britain is to become great again and Western culture is to survive long into the future it will depend largely on our children understanding mathematics and that, as you've probably realised by now, is where you come in as an educator. The world is changing exponentially and the possibilities are endless. It is time to lay the foundations for generations to come to and ensure our legacy of solid ground on which to build a basecamp from which the universe could be explored.

Mathematics, for me, should be the essence of simplicity and when done correctly is both straightforward and transparent. While it may too appear mysterious and complex to many people, when the opportunities are made accessible there really isn't much our pupils can't get their head around, so there should be no excuses for anyone in the education profession.

That, as you will have garnered from the title, is where this book comes into play. Neurologists will tell you that the human brain makes connections between synapses during the learning process and the greater the number of connections the deeper the understanding and strength of information recall. These connections are created through the shared experiences of the body's senses so it makes sense that pupils should be given the opportunity to truly experience mathematics and this includes making mistakes or drawing misconceptions. The number one rule in my own classroom is that I'm interested in how you got there, not where you are and that it is okay to make mistakes. I cannot stress this enough and it forms the basis of every maths related conversation I have in and out of the classroom. Not only do the children feel safe but they understand that making mistakes and misunderstanding is a prerequisite for learning. Misconceptions are only one step away from correctly formed concepts if harnessed with care and skill.

It is true that these skills take years to develop and that over time it will become second nature, to this I can attest. Only, though, if you are willing to do the ground work and (re)define your behaviour patterns. It must become your sole aim to treat misconceptions as a pivotal point in the learning journey. At times they can, and must, be prevented but more often than not they should be identified and addressed. Within these three different but equal stages we can find the structure of our narrative and the journey we will embark on together. Initially we will discuss the importance of preventing misconceptions through what we say, do and present to the children. There are some misconceptions which are unforgivable yet unmistakably prevalent throughout English primary schools and we must do everything we can to prevent them from occurring. Part I of this book will make that clear.

It will also try to identify the language with which topics should be approached and the nuances in our preconceptions. The 2014 National Curriculum places high importance on the consistency of language used when approaching mathematical concepts and rightly so. This cannot be stressed enough and I will make it my *raison d'être* to relay this as clearly and relevantly as possible in the coming pages. The initial chapters of this book will identify common misconceptions and explain exactly how to prepare each concept accurately so that it may provide a foundation on which subsequent learning can be build. Subject knowledge is essential if we are to have any chance of developing outstanding teaching and learning in our classrooms. To accelerate pupil progress class teacher subject knowledge must be first class and nothing less. Subject knowledge fosters understanding, addresses misconceptions, fosters understanding, contributes to effective differentiation, fosters understanding, gives the class teacher a much needed confidence/presence in the classroom and, most importantly, fosters understanding.

Improper use of repetition perhaps but we have known for a long time that a sound, relational understanding of mathematics is a key focus, as outlined by Skemp (1976), of education professionals across the globe and the foundation upon which this book has been built. Which is why it pains me to say that, in 2014, we may still have the misfortune of encountering education professionals who suggest it is okay to 'just teach children the tricks to get by' and ask 'why do they need understanding anyway?' Shocking I know! I almost choked on my coffee when I came across this for the first time. So much so that it altered the opening of this book because I cannot stress enough how important it is that children understand the mathematics they encounter.

Then as we continue into Part II we will see examples of common misconceptions and how they can be addressed in a classroom situation. This will form the main bulk of the content within these pages and act as a guide to the given progression in mathematics. I would recommend you make yourself aware of what is expected across the curriculum, particularly the years directly above and below your own. Something which will take your maths teaching to greater depths and provide you with the tools to turn every maths lesson into a potential eureka moment. I highly recommend that when you are planning you dip in and out where necessary, concepts will often overlap but this is only in the interest of providing a comprehensive guide to this particular progression in primary mathematics learning.

While it may seem like great teachers need to be able to predict the future, many analogies can be drawn with chess. It appears that the grand masters are able to see 10-15 moves into the future when really it's a matter of 2 or 3 moves at most. In this way the classroom teacher will be able to see the common misconceptions, where they originate from and how they link to the current misconception on offer during their lesson. Patterns have a way of repeating and misconceptions are no exception. It may often be a case that the use of particular strategies or language will create the optimum conditions but certainly the 2014 curriculum is an interesting document, whether you agree with its progression or not, and should provide a high degree of value for anyone willing to delve further and explore. Remember, the following pages are the sum total of my experience and research thus far. I, as you should too, reserve the right to change my mind when better, more insightful evidence comes to light. The practitioner willing to ensure their subject knowledge is the best it can be is the practitioner serving their pupils in the best way possible. Content and pedagogy matter and can be hugely interesting. The responsibility and the opportunity are yours. Now is the time to take it.

Reference

Skemp, R. (1976) 'Relational Understanding and Instrumental Understanding', *Mathematics Teaching*, 77: 20-26.

Part I
Common misconceptions

1 Common misconceptions

Diamonds are forever unclear

With hundreds of millions of card decks sold each year there's a fairly good chance you've seen the 14th century French playing cards that have become somewhat commonplace, certainly in Western Europe, over the last seven or eight hundred years. Perhaps I'm being overly specific in my description but I want to be sure that when I talk about playing cards you know exactly to what it is I am referring. You see when I use the term it is my intention to describe the playing cards used in games that are known colloquially as hearts or chase the lady, solitaire or patience, rummy or gin rummy and even the more competitive poker and blackjack, sometimes known as pontoon or 21. Usually they come in standard 52 card decks, of which approximately one quarter, not counting joker and instruction cards of course, are adorned with what we are led to believe are two-dimensional representations of metastable allotropes of carbon.

Yet, no matter how much you want to believe the seemingly trustworthy merchants who brought the cards to our shores all those centuries ago, there is no officially recognised two-dimensional diamond. It doesn't quite have the same ring to it in a card playing context but a rhombus on the other hand is defined as a non-self-intersecting quadrilateral with sides of equal length. Where the angles are 60 degrees the shape may colloquially be known as a diamond and where 45 degrees, a lozenge but there is no standard. It is worth noting a square is also a non-self-intersecting quadrilateral with equal sides and that the word diamond is frowned upon as a common misconception at Key Stage 3.

All of this information is easily accessible from a well-known online encyclopaedia but that isn't even remotely the point.[1] If you do one thing other than read this book I urge you to search for the forum post 'Diamonds are forever unclear'.[2] A selection of posts regarding the illustrious nature of the lesser spotted rhombus, it provides an example of how interesting and absorbing shape, space and measure can be as a branch of mathematics. The problem is too many professionals, myself included for a long time, consider shape and space to be a list of general knowledge facts, of little mathematical importance that are to be taught with little to no forethought and planning.

How wrong we all are, or were, I can't quite be certain of the tense in which this most common of foibles exists! This one section of conversation, aligned with possibly the greatest maths related blog post title in history, serves to provide evidence of the controversial and sometimes chequered past of shape and space. In real terms, shape and space is the Steve McQueen of mathematical content areas. We've all heard of 'Bullet', we all know a car went fast down a hill, but we don't really know much else other than that and we've never really taken the time to get to know him. The same can be said for shape and space. Do you honestly believe you can extend and deepen your pupils' understanding, as per the statutory requirements of the 2014 National Curriculum, in the same way you could in number? Do you feel confident enough to extend your most able mathematicians beyond the scope of your year group? Do you believe your teaching of shape and space is engaging and inspiring? If the answer to any of these questions is yes then I doff my proverbial hat.

If you answered no to any of the questions then now is the time to take action. The National Centre for Excellence in the Teaching of Mathematics, NCETM, and nrich.maths.org have both taken great strides towards the provision of greater depth and challenge in light of ever changing demands of the education system. Access to either of their websites will put you a few clicks away from the acquisition of the knowledge and guidance you need to truly rejuvenate your mathematics teaching.[3] Now there's a very good chance you are at the beginning of your teaching career and haven't had the opportunity to reach this level of regret at opportunities missed in the past. You are in the fortuitous position of having the opportunity to write your own story from scratch. Why not champion shape and space? Take the bull by the horns and inspire those around you to do the same.

When considering the impact you can have I strongly recommend you consider the real life application of the content you wish to disseminate, in this particular case what is generally known as shape and space. As the aims of the 2014 National Curriculum explain reasonably clearly and succinctly, *mathematics is an interconnected subject in which pupils need to be able to move fluently between representations of mathematical ideas*. This fluency will only come about with proper planning and consideration of the wider connotations of this interconnectivity and the role it has to play in our lives. Ask yourself if, as an example, understanding the properties of a cube can serve a greater, more meaningful and relevant purpose, or is it a stepping stone to greater and deeper understanding, perhaps even a pivotal stopping point on the road map of mathematics education. It may be all of these things, it may even be none, but you, as facilitator of learning, should make it your priority to ensure that you have given sufficient consideration to the possibility.

This opening section is brimming with some of my favourite mathematical controversies. Feel free to borrow them but most importantly take on the mantle and find your own, develop them and mould the curriculum into something that will allow you to inspire in the way you've always dreamed you could.

How many sides does a circle have?

With that in mind I think we should look at one of my personal favourites and a guaranteed mind-blower, particularly with children aged 9–11. Technically the information I plan to impart is still up for debate but the most philosophical of mathematical problems can be the most interesting, diverse and inspirational problems to be found in our universe. The circle is up there with $1 = 0.9999999 \ldots$ in the upper echelons of mathematical problems. If we could personify them, or even deify them, they'd be Zeus and Orpheus. Such is the regal lineage of these factoids.

It must be noted that I've not found any practical application for this in the classroom other than encouraging children to challenge the mathematical knowledge handed down to them but it's definitely worthy of an appearance on *QI*. A typical conversation might go something like this ...

Adult A: How many sides does a circle have?
Adult B: That's easy. One curved side. (Folds arms defiantly)
Adult A: Try again.
Adult B: Look, here is a circle, it has one curved side.
Adult A: In actual fact a circle has an infinite number of straight sides.
Adult B: (Slumps to the floor following brief but intense brain explosion)
Adult A: (Goes off to find a mop and bucket)

Alternatively Adult B could express disagreement with your statement through the application of a range of gestures or use of the local vernacular but there are a number of reasons why a circle is considered to have an infinite number of straight lines. Alas, such a rare creature is the mathematics graduate who has chosen to pursue a career in primary education that it may be detrimental to my intentions to provide a purely mathematical explanation. Allow me, however, to try and clarify my proposition.

A circle is made of an infinite number of points. A line or a side is made by joining 2 points. If there are infinite points there will be infinite lines that can be made by joining 2 points. A circle, thus, has an infinite number of sides.

Granted, the relevance of this information is miniscule in relation to other topics covered in this book but if not to prepare our pupils for a future in mathematics it can be used to encourage mathematical reasoning and deduction. Try the conversation out on a group of children and allow the pupils to guide the discussion. I have no doubt you'll be amazed where you end up. After all, my intention is to inspire greater understanding and as we all know dialogue and investigation are cornerstones in the development of relational understanding.

I must also add that there is a lot of debate surrounding this as a circle is not officially classed as a polygon but there is a school of thought which believes that as the number of sides approaches infinity the polygon becomes closer to looking like a circle. If you're not working during your summer holidays you may even want to search for information on notions such as the Jordan Curve Theorem, the area and perimeter of polygons with an infinite number of sides or you may wish to spend time with your family, the choice is yours.

2-D shapes are not 3-D shapes

It may seem blatantly obvious and I expect you'd like to see my credentials at this point but, trust me; all is not what it seems. I dare say in every school in the country there sits at least one tray of resources, hidden in plain sight and utterly brazen in their defiance of mathematical convention, bearing the label '2-D shapes'. Their use is widespread and I have no doubt they were labelled with the best of intentions but when all is said and done 2-D shapes have two dimensions. They are two dimensional. They cannot be picked up. They cannot be collected in boxes and used as a practical resource and, if you want to be extremely pedantic, they cannot be drawn on an interactive white board, such are the geometrical properties of the surface.

This, though ostensibly difficult to comprehend, is a very simple premise which defines their very being and lays the foundations of our understanding of the universe. *2-D shapes are two dimensional 2-D = 2 dimensions.* Yet this apparently elementary principle is seemingly overlooked in primary classrooms the world over for reasons unknown. Your job now is to find your maths coordinator, hunt down every mislabelled box or tray and prevent an easily avoidable misconception in the making. Call them *3 dimensional representations of 2 dimensional shapes*, *3-D shapes*, *3 dimensional shapes*, call them whatever you like (except 2-D shapes of course) but please do not actively seek to immerse children in an inaccurate environment with incorrect vocabulary which will only have a lasting effect on their concept development for years to come.

Why should we worry about this? What harm does it do?

Well, in the more immediate future, those children will be in your class and one or more will look admiringly towards you holding a 3-D shape with properties covering all three dimensions. Yet with which they have attached a two-dimensional meaning. For example ...

Child: Look, a rectangle.
Adult: That's not a rectangle, that's a cuboid.
Child: No it's not. It looks like a rectangle. Look! (Child points to rectangular face)
Adult: This shape has depth, it cannot be a rectangle.
Child: But it was in the 2-D shape tray.
Adult: ....

... and because there is nothing you can say in retort, the child has you hand over fist and you only have yourself to blame.

In the longer term, these children will be in charge of your twilight years. A terrifying thought indeed. All being well they'll develop an advanced understanding of shape and space, honing the basic conceptual understanding you fostered, and will eventually apply their knowledge of shape and space to the buildings you inhabit and the structures you use on a daily basis. If you want your walls to stay upright, your bridges to reach from one piece of land to the other and support the weight of hundreds of cars I suggest you get a move on with that relabelling.

Something I've noticed since taking the leap into fatherhood, an event which perhaps unwisely coincided with the writing of this book, is the plethora of material available online which reinforces this most torrid of misconceptions, creeping into our homes at night and misinforming our children right under our noses. If you have embraced, or wish to embrace, technology then I suggest you treat it as you would treat any resource in your classroom. Ensure that you have prepared thoroughly beforehand, understand the content that will be delivered via the chosen medium and make certain that there isn't a cylinder jumping up and down purporting to be a circle. If you don't not only will you have shot yourself in the foot but you'll pre-empt any potential domestic disputes with your significant other as to the relevance of your argument and insistence that the cylinder be exterminated post-haste.

A triangle can't be upside down

Now, as we all know, the internal angles of a triangle total 180 degrees, they are three in total, as are the sides and the corners too. This is the definition. Orientation, however, unless you are trying to get to grips with bottom up leadership models, is never mentioned. Yet there are children who believe that a right-angled triangle as shown in Figure 1.1 or the equilateral triangle shown in Figure 1.2 are the one true representation of each. How can it be? What is happening that this, in the 21st century, is the case?

The mathematics, in this particular example, comes a mere second to the questions raised about provision of opportunity and pedagogical perspective/outlook by this occurrence. We must ask ourselves why so many children are allowed the time to cement such misinformed conclusions, why they are not corrected and what has happened in the intervening period between the introduction of the triangle and this realisation of the limited scope possessed by the children in your care.

They should, using accurate two-dimensional representations, have been given the opportunity to explore shape and develop an enquiry based approach to new learning from

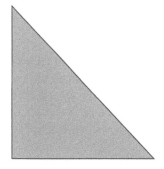

Figure 1.1

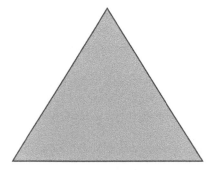

Figure 1.2

the youngest of ages. And while it is preferable that the Early Years model be adopted throughout the primary school and beyond, I realise this will rarely be the case. Yet, during those formative early years, were they encouraged to question everything and was time taken to provide alternative orientation during adult structured and child initiated learning? Whether you had any control over this or not you should hopefully realise the direction I am heading with this particular example. Your responsibility is to ensure the depth and breadth of the curriculum is unsurpassed and that pupils are able to manipulate and apply knowledge with fluency. To do so they will have to have been taught to question and they will have to have been given a varied and rich diet of opportunity which would indeed include triangles and rhombuses in a variety of orientations.

In the classroom this could take various forms depending on what is, and what you make, available. For instance you could choose to have shapes represented on the interactive whiteboard in a range of orientations, pupils could then sort them without altering said orientation with discussion around properties and how they remain constant regardless of their positioning. You may choose to use isometric paper when drawing shapes and have predetermined points which you know will provide a range of possible orientations or you may even, quite simply, choose to present the shapes in different ways in your classroom displays. Even if the display has no relevance to shape the work may be displayed within the confines of the shapes and pupils are allowed to familiarise themselves with the reality that shapes conform just as little as children, and adults for that matter, do. The key, as it always seems, lies in the preparation and consideration given by you and your colleagues.

Ruler and rule

I was once told that a ruler is actually called a rule but when I did some research it turned out that while this once may have been the case, the two words are now recognised as interchangeable by the *Oxford English Dictionary* and that's good enough for me. Perhaps the confusion came from the origins of the word but the more I think about it the less likely it seems. At the very least it's an interesting, albeit brief, journey for the etymological anoraks amongst us.

In the beginning there was Latin and to the speakers of Latin the instrument used for measuring (usually a stick, sticks are good at measuring) was known as a *regula*. A few centuries later the Old French for similar measuring sticks became *reuler* and eventually Middle English developed the word rule. It is possible that somewhere down the line people began to pronounce the 'er' in *reuler*, forgetting momentarily that the French don't pronounce many of their word endings, and usage became so popular that the lexicon was altered irrevocably.

Language, particularly the English language, is a unique cocktail of patterns and guidelines, a marriage of many tongues and perhaps it's best not to question the origins of every word. In terms of mathematical understanding there are but three simple steps to follow:

1   Choose one of the words - rule or ruler - I don't mind which, just choose *one*.
2   Everyone in school uses the same word.
3   Ask everyone who ignores step 2 to read step 1 again.

1:2 is not the same as ½

I've not encountered this particular misnomer first hand but I'm told it can be quite a common occurrence for children to grow up in the belief that the ratio 1:2 is the same as ½. Let's use orange squash as an example.

You wake up. You decide to have a glass of squash. You decide to dilute your squash with water. An everyday series of decisions indeed but wait, how do we get the perfect balance of water and squash? Weak squash tastes like water (ugh) and strong squash makes your eyes pop and facial features draw inwards at a rate of knots. After a few seconds of online research you find that a ratio of 1:2 will create the optimum conditions for refreshment. Problem solved. For every one part squash you will need to add two parts water. Let's say your glass is 300ml. That's 100ml of squash, 200ml of water. Delicious!

Now, let's imagine you think that 1:2 is the same as ½. You repeat the earlier stages of the decision making process but misinterpret the ratio. Still using the 300ml glass, you opt for 150ml of squash, 150ml of water. It's only when you take a large swig and tears begin to stream down your cheeks while a dry gargling sound escapes from the place which used to produce words that you realise something has gone horribly wrong.

To deliver this particular concept with the desired accuracy you must establish the vocabulary you intend to use. The ratio is the association between two or more quantities. The ratio 3:2 recognises the associated rate of 3 for every 2 e.g. 3 metres for every 2 minutes. Ratios can be equivalent and sometimes you can refer to the above ratio as 3 to 2. I personally would stick to the use of 3 for every 2 until the pupils are secure in their understanding. It is imperative you explore the terms association, quantities, equivalence and the phrase 'for every'. If you do this you will have started to lay the foundations of a solid understanding of ratio and proportion. Sometimes it is worth presenting misconceptions as your own ideas; we should be modelling how we deal with such occurrences after all, and perhaps you could record a ratio as a fraction. Do the children notice? Can you address it with the explanation given above or similar? I would suggest yes and implore you to do so.

When taking mathematical accuracy into consideration I would hasten to add that ratio is the quantitative relation between two amounts showing the number of times one value contains or is contained within another. Proportion on the other hand, a term which is often married with ratio, is a part, share or number considered in comparative relation to a whole. This subtle distinction must be drawn in order that pupils can reason accurately and succinctly. Such are our mathematical ambitions for them.

Greater or bigger?

One of the most frequently erroneous and contestable facets of teacher/pupil dialogue involves the often interchangeable language of comparison and relativity. In my experience it is as common to hear 'Is it greater or less than 5?' as it is to hear someone ask 'Is it bigger or smaller than 5?' I have always been instructed to use the language greater than and less than, and any other derivatives of the root words great and less, to describe the relationship between numbers. Yet I find it difficult to incontrovertibly explain why. I know that the Primary National Strategy made reference to the term greater, but it also included a description of bigger numbers and reference to the term smaller so it is unclear as to where this opinion came from, if indeed it originated in the late 1990s at all.

I feel the subtle nuances in the English language make the terms greater and less than more suitable for comparison of number because bigger and smaller are so often associated with measurements, particularly height. In some dictionaries, such as the online Cambridge dictionaries, greater than is defined as a specialised term for describing the difference between amounts, while no such definition exists for bigger than. I would ensure that any explanations of how you intend to use the vocabulary remain clear and precise and as such create a clear stance towards the vocabulary of greater and less than. It may not be a case of mathematical accuracy but it is certainly a case of increased linguistic accuracy – one that will help pupils in their formative years and could perhaps be used as a discussion point for those sharpening their reasoning skills.

As pupils hone their reasoning skills it is essential that we provide them with the necessary language, a veritable vocabulary bank if you will, from which they can withdraw on demand to express themselves as clearly and concisely as possible when solving mathematical problems or explaining mathematical concepts and equations. Very often we can be tempted to use the words at our disposal but there are terms which have been designed over centuries to describe the very concepts we wish to explain. The possibilities for your pupils, regardless of their age or developmental level, are endless if we take the time to prepare the language we wish to disseminate. If they are exposed to higher order mathematical terms consistently over an extended period of time then they will begin to use the terms independently and understanding will move towards a more relational state much more quickly.

The language of calculation

As far back as I can remember children have always been offered 'lists of sums' to do and I'm sure I've worked through my own fair share. I did, however, think that this use of language was reserved for teachers in the slightly hazy and possibly rose-tinted colloquial Ireland of my school days. Imagine my disappointment when I discovered how mistaken I was about the prevalence of such inaccurate dissemination. As *you* establish the expectations in your class each year it is essential to introduce the language of calculation early. There are distinct pieces of vocabulary used to describe the outcome of each of the four operations and they have been chosen for their adept ability to simultaneously engender both the process and the outcome they refer to. As we know it takes around two years for language to be assimilated so the earlier, the better.

The sum does exist as a mathematical term but not how it was described to me all those years ago. Instead a sum describes the total when two or more numbers/objects are added together e.g. the sum of 2 + 5 is 7. When calculating we are said to be finding the sum. This is common for all the operations and examples will hark back to this continually. Addition = sum = finding the sum.

When subtracting, and I much prefer the term subtract to take away though both are mathematically accurate, the remaining quantity is known as the difference. We are said to be finding the difference between two or more numbers/objects. Subtraction = difference =

finding the difference. It is highly likely the word difference was chosen for its French origins, difference being the present participle of *differre - to set apart*. It makes sense to me that on a very literal level we are setting apart the two quantities to identify the difference. The actuality may be much more straightforward but this particular example sits well with me at present. Pupils are not, as I have heard before, making one number smaller; this is rife with inaccuracy and reeks of a lack of subject knowledge on the part of the teacher where sufficient foresight has not been employed to see the difficulty it will cause as pupils progress through their educational careers. The numbers aren't being made smaller; we are finding the difference.

When multiplying, again I prefer multiplication to times, the total is known as the product, derived from the Latin *productum, to bring forth*. We are said to be finding the product. Multiplication = product = finding the product.

When dividing the remaining quantity is known as the quotient. It is considerably less prevalent in its use but of equal importance to the earnest mathematics teacher. As in the other examples we are said to be finding the quotient. Division = quotient = finding the quotient. Quite simply this is a derivation from the Latin *quotiens* which translates, as you would expect, to *how many times* and refers specifically to the number of times a number will fit inside another, greater, number.

While describing these essential terms I alluded that I preferred the use of subtraction over take away and multiply over times. I agree that the latter in each example serve to describe the function they are related to, we are indeed taking a quantity away and making reference to the number of times we add the same number, but there is no reason why the mathematically accurate terms cannot foster a similar resonance with the by-product of increased mathematical accuracy. One day the Latin based descriptions may be replaced by more modern and relevant examples but until that time it is abundantly clear we must remain true to our guiding principles of mathematical accuracy. Pupils, in my experience, will gravitate towards the more colloquial times and take away but it's your responsibility as a champion of all things accurate to correct, model and explain vocabulary choices.

When teaching calculation it is often expected that vocabulary remain in a place of prominence so that pupils may refer constantly but there are other strategies you may want to consider. The use of an average football labelled with stickers adorned in key mathematical vocabulary can be an engaging way to encourage pupils to reflect on the meaning of essential terms. The ball can be carefully thrown around the classroom with selected pupils required to coin a definition of the term closest to their thumb. I find this particularly useful when developing an understanding of the language of calculation. You may also want to ask your pupils to create the aforementioned display in order that some relevance can be brought to the definitions we want them to retain. A list of definitions can only go so far, the essence of the words must be meaningful and pertinent to the pupils.

The commutative laws

In addition to the aforementioned definitions it is important that pupils realise and understand the relationships that exist within the four operations. This stems from one of the more frequent misconceptions, often seen in the work of children of approximately 7 or

8 who, as they begin to explore the operations in greater formality, naturally experiment with concepts. The manifestation usually takes the form of an *upside down* columnar subtraction or something akin to 3 ÷ 9 = 3 and while not strictly the by-product of adult intervention we can take steps to address the misconceptions through the use of language and description.

It was a visit to schools in Shanghai, and one student explanation in particular, that made the importance of the laws abundantly clear to me. When explaining how he had been taught to calculate at school he went to great lengths to explain the commutative, associative and distributive laws.

Where numbers are commutative they are interchangeable and an identical outcome is achieved no matter the order of the calculation. For instance 5 + 4 and 4 + 5 will have identical sums in the same way the product of 5 × 4 will be identical to that of 4 × 5. The numbers are able to commute freely with no consequence. Where children often go awry is that they believe the commutative law applies to subtraction and division. They must be taught that this is not the case and accurate marking and feedback can address this quite easily. If the operation in question is explained and suitable reference made to the actual and physical process, not only will the method have greater relevance but this common misconception can be addressed with minimal fuss.

Anecdotally, I have found great success when taking account of these laws when teaching methods of calculation. During each session I would provide pupils with a question and ask them to show me how they would solve it. Not only would this provide me with starting points from which to take each child but it allows me to model the desired next step and to reference the link between the operations. I would explain the best way to check that we have been accurate is to use the inverse and ask the pupils to show me how they would do so. This clearly provides a unified approach to calculation whereby each is a key component of the other. I have even heard others say that there are only two operations, multiplication/division and addition/subtraction, and I believe there is a certain amount of truth in this. As such I would highly recommend you take the commutative laws into account before, during and after every such lesson.

The meaning of =

There are many mathematical symbols of importance but none encounters greater disservice than the equals sign. The symmetrical embodiment of its own modest sentiment, I have heard many words attributed to the meaning of this particular symbol, each more inaccurate than the last. There's a good chance you've heard it said yourself that a calculation *makes, leaves* or *gives you* an answer when in all actuality it does not have the ability to do any such thing. The symbol is known as the equals sign because its primary role is to identify and demarcate equivalence in the mathematical world in which it exists: 9 + 5 = 14 is the same as saying nine add five is the same as or is equal to fourteen. Equally we could say that 9 + 5 = 10 + 4 as the = symbol sits amid a balanced equation where both sides are equal to the other. Wherever you see that symbol be sure to express the accurate meaning. *The same as* is acceptable, as is *equal to*, but be sure not to cheapen the mathematics with *makes, leaves, gives you* and any other incongruence.

1 isn't a prime number - composite crime

It's not entirely clear if anyone still believes that 1 is a prime number any more but such is the nature of the rollercoaster relationship between 1 and the other prime numbers that as close as 2011 it was purported that it was indeed still a prime number despite being written off as early as 400 BCE. The standard definition of a prime number usually refers to the fact that a prime number is a number which has only two factors, 1 and itself. By this very definition one is excluded from the prime numbers yet it has a greater role to play and thus, there are more meaningful reasons for its exclusion from this exclusive sequence of numbers. What was once known as the units is now known as the ones. However, this really racks up the reasoning against the consideration of 1 as a prime number. This position of class makes it a 'divisor of unity ... a number with ... multiplicative inverse' and creates a need for care when using the number 1 and most importantly for 2 to become the first prime number. If it cannot be reduced, as all primes must, then it is clear for us to see where the classification must eventually fall for good.

If you are mathematically inclined, in as much as the world you see appears in code rather than images, and have the resources, I understand a cool $1,000,000 (approximately £700,918.24, 67,578,950 Indian Rupees or 6,579,550 Chinese Yuan if you were wondering) is on offer to anyone who can solve any of the seven classic mathematical problems puzzling mathematicians around the globe. The Clay Mathematics Institute's Millennium Prize was announced in 2000 and features a greatly reduced field from the 23 problems discussed in 1900. Anyone brave enough to take on the challenges should be prepared to try to describe all solutions in whole numbers (Birch and Swinnerton-Dyer Conjecture), wrestle with quantum physics (Yang-Mills and Mass Gap), glue together some pretty advanced geometric concepts (Hodge Conjecture), explain the behaviour of waves and air currents when they react with boats and jets respectively (Navier-Stokes Equation), sort groups of students in a way no current supercomputer can (P vs NP Problem), bend the rules of the second and third dimensions with rubber bands, though that's actually been solved but it sounds fun (Poincaré Conjecture), and even find a succinct description for the distribution of prime numbers (Riemann Hypothesis). And while one has already been solved, that still leaves $6,000,000 up for grabs, and who knows your pupils may even go on to solve one or two of them.

My point is, while we were on the subject of prime numbers, that you may be doing your pupils a disservice by not opening them up to such possibilities. Everyone knows what a Nobel Prize is but do they know what the Fields Medal and the Abel Prize are? Have they heard of Simon Donaldson, Timothy Gowers, Richard Borcherds or Alan Baker? All notable British mathematicians and potential role models for our pupils waiting to be uncovered and celebrated for their contribution to mathematics.

I once heard that it took 14 computers several years to find a new prime number and that the men behind the idea were awarded, funnily enough, $1,000,000, which leads me to believe there may be a benefactor masquerading as a wealthy donor when in actual fact he doesn't expect anyone to solve the problems he's dishing out, but I could not confirm or refute this tale. The *New York Times* did report on 21 January 2016 that the greatest of the prime numbers was in actual fact found by a computer in the University of Central Missouri (Chang, 2016). Weighing in at a staggering 22 million digits it is the 15th such number to be found using the

Mersenne search techniques and took PC No. 5 as it is known 31 days to complete the necessary calculation. It is reported that it would take 3 months to record by hand and fill 6,000 or 7,000 sheets of paper, depending on point size. This alone is a fact I intend to share with every Key Stage 2 class I teach for the sheer fact that it requires little to no mathematical knowledge to understand that this is impressive stuff and then maybe, just maybe, they'll begin to think that if prime numbers can be this impressive then perhaps this is something they might want to get involved in. You'll be pleased to know PC No. 5 has now happily retired.

Counting

It should go without saying that counting is an essential skill and, for me and many others that I know and have worked with, pupils should be given the opportunity to count every day. The more specific and appropriate the focus the more conducive to progress perhaps but certainly it must be regular and consistent. The different stages that have come to define how we learn to count have long been highlighted as a progression and while it is not my intention to regurgitate the plethora of research regarding the how and why of counting, it is my intention to discuss the possible misconceptions and how to alleviate them. I very often naively set out initially to claim that counting is not saying number names and there have been many occasions during which I have lectured my pupils on that very theme when really it should be a case that counting is not *merely* saying number names.

That is, however, the essence of naivety as you often don't realise until it is too late. Luckily on this occasion I have had a chance to continuously review my learning and understanding in an ongoing process of professional development, something which is afforded to all practitioners and I cannot stress enough the importance of taking time to reflect on your practice in the now before it passes you by, the weekend comes along and all has been forgotten and an opportunity slips through your metaphorical fingers.

This has allowed me to make a subtle modification that really makes all the difference to the content of this particular sub-section. For the practitioner teaching children to count or facilitating counting it is important that they are aware of the difference between recitation and enumeration as outlined by Thompson (1995a, 1995b). He makes it abundantly clear that the recitation of number names is an important precursor to what is known colloquially as counting. This enumeration (the association of a number with a given set of objects), as he rightly points out, is not possible if there is a limit to which you can count. I cannot count four cubes if I can only recite the numbers 1–3.

It is essential, however, that you make this as clear to your pupils as Thompson did for us all. They must be in no doubt that the recitation of number names is a forerunner of enumeration and that concrete and abstract connections must be made in order that pupils develop this most important of skills. I would recommend the *counting stick,* often a metre stick with ten clear divisions as shown in Figure 1.3, as the primary method of teaching children to count and recall number sequences. Yes it is important that we progress through

Figure 1.3

the developmental stages of counting, via circles, by touching, without touching, pointing etc., but for me it is the embodiment of the literal and abstract union, the alliance of the left and right hemispheres of the brain.

For a visual dose of professional development YouTube contains many videos, some from the 'ATM' and the now archived 'Teachers TV', which offer an interesting insight into the range of uses for the counting stick. If you search for the link 'Times Tables in 10 minutes' you'll find a fantastic example of the counting stick in action with the 17 times table. This particular example encompasses many of the approaches that can be used to draw out mathematical dialogue while developing use of those essential models and images and while times tables may be the focus the strategies deployed in this example can act as a starting point for your considerations. At the very least I would recommend all maths leaders to share this with staff as part of a school wide approach in order that high quality counting can take place on a daily basis.

There is a wealth of video material available for free online which could certainly contribute to your own daily development, even if it is just for five or ten minutes at a time. Once you've watch 'Times Tables in 10 minutes' I have no doubt you'll be inspired and keen to delve into the search for further viewing. Who knows where the search may take you! Yet I digress.

When we allow children to count and provide opportunity for them to progress through the developmental stages we will often find familiar misconceptions which we must address through continued discussion and modelling. The opportunity to orally address misconceptions when counting is gift laden and key to the mathematical understanding of the children involved. Executed correctly, not only can progress be accelerated but the foundations strengthened indefinitely as well.

You will often find the first recognised misconception, *words omitted,* in very young children who, when they count, will leave out a number in sequence e.g. six, seven, nine, ten. This is not limited strictly to younger children but it can be addressed early on with regular use of the counting stick and opportunities to attribute names to numbers early on. Similar strategies will alleviate any issues with *words in the wrong order* and *words repeated.* They will even pre-empt any difficulties found when not starting from the *beginning* of a sequence, moulding the plasticity of their young minds to be prepared for counting whatever shape or form it may take. Much like the example, you could choose to label the divisions on the counting stick, removing them as understanding of the sequence develops, or ask pupils to label them with you. It may even be a case of pupils rearranging the labels or placing a given number of items beside the divisions to represent the number. You can do anything really, certainly anything you feel will take pupils from the concrete, to the pictorial and eventually on towards the abstract model the counting stick is intended to be.

Equally importantly, and easily addressed through the activities and strategies outlined above, are the *errors of analogy* our minds make in their attempts to piece together the facts on offer into an overarching concept which makes sense to all levels of the brain. Examples may include thirteen, fourteen, fiveteen or thirty-eight, thirty-nine, thirty-ten and it is here where discussion can be used to push on the thinking of those children who can already count, through explanation and reasoning, and those children with clear gaps can be taught the correct patterns to follow. I don't think I've met a child who didn't at some point confuse this issue, in the same way we commonly struggle with the bridge between 100 and 101, etc. A sweeping statement perhaps and I would love to meet the child who hasn't but in general I feel we can be sure that the misconceptions outlined are rather commonplace, developmental stepping-stones you might say, which you can be prepared for and can deal with in a fitting and timely matter. Remember, if misconceptions are addressed immediately then progress is accelerated and understanding deepened.

Face value, place value, numeral, number, digit

Mathematical terms can often be used interchangeably with devastating consequences so it is best practice to ensure that what you say is as accurate as is humanly possible. Now, as you may have inferred, I don't pretend to be an omnipotent being but I do try my hardest to ensure the language I disseminate is accurate and meaningful and will ultimately contribute to the betterment of my pupils' reasoning and understanding.

With that in mind there are several terms which we as practitioners must use with such precision that our pupils have no choice but to use them correctly as well. I was lucky enough to pose a problem involving these terms to a group of colleagues in Year 6 and Year 2 and while I am certain everyone knew what the terms meant, there was a certain amount of indecision when it came to staking a claim to the actual definition. This is not a slight on my colleagues, far from it, my only intention is to highlight the sentiment of teachers across the country who acknowledge that there is an urgent need to ensure that we are all fully aware of exactly what we are teaching and the language that must be used. If you use the following guide as a basis for your use of the terms included then you will have started on the righteous mathematical path.

The all important terms

- *Face value* is the value printed or depicted *(on a coin or bank note for instance)*.
- *Place value* is the numerical value a digit has by virtue of its position in a number.
- *Numerals* are letters, figures, words, parts of speech expressing or denoting a number/numbers.
- Digit – a whole number less than 10; any of the ten Arabic numerals representing 0–9.
- The term 'Number' happens to have three possible definitions:
  - something which graphically or symbolically represents a numerical quantity, as a word, figure, or group of these.
  - an abstract entity representing a quantity, used to express how many things are being referred to, or how much there is of some thing or property; an arithmetical value corresponding to a particular quantity of something.
  - an analogous entity or value used in mathematical operations without reference to actual things.

The subtlety is palpable but with this handy guide you can ensure that your offering is as accurate as possible.

Nil, null, nought, nothing, nada, zilch - zero as a proper name and place holder

There are many colloquialisms bandied about when discussing the use of zero. Depending on geographic location they can vary widely yet still attempt to represent the same crucial mathematical concept. Mathematically speaking I recommend you stick to zero, a derivation that has travelled to the English language from North Africa via Italy and France, because, as we have previously discussed with other concepts, there are too many social contexts attributed to the other variations. Zilch for instance echoes thoughts of money, nil with football and several other net games, oh with telephone number recitation and nada with something that cannot be found.

At a primary level we are concerned largely with the emptiness of zero, empty being the pre-Islamic origin of the word. For us, it is a place holder first and foremost. When calculating zero represents the idea of emptiness and is used to express the size numbers e.g. the powers of 10. Using the aforementioned column method of addition and subtraction, where a class is devoid of value, such as the tens in 105, zero is used to signify this lack of value. When we multiply using the grid method it is used to signify the size of the numbers once partitioned. When teaching these methods it is key you use the language place holder to ensure pupils are able to verbalise their thinking.

As we draw the first section to a close, a section in which we have handled some delicate and potentially contentious issues as carefully as is possible without banality, I would like you to consider the possibilities for zero as children progress through the education system. There are many more applications and uses we have not considered because they are either not relevant or would prove so absorbing that the true point of this book may be lost. If anything it is hoped that I have been able to open doors previously hidden. Doors to the subjective and argumentative side of mathematics that is often overlooked. I use these terms in the most positive way possible, for a lack of argument and opinion would create a stale vacuum that will serve no purpose in the progression of mathematics teaching. Here, the torch has been lit, as it has by many before me, take the torch, run with it and devise routines and systems which allow you to prepare sufficiently for the challenges you must provide your children with. The mathematical baton is in play and you are the relay runner!

Notes

1 https://en.wikipedia.org/wiki/Diamond_(disambiguation).
2 http://mathforum.org/library/drmath/view/76247.html.
3 www.NCETM.org.uk and www.nrich.maths.org.

Bibliography

Caldwell, C.K. (n.d.) 'Why is the number one not prime?' *Prime Pages FAQ*, https://primes.utm.edu/notes/faq/one.html (accessed 30 April 2016).
Caldwell, C.K., Reddick, A. and Xiong, Y. (2012) 'The history of the primality of one: a selection of sources', *Journal of Integer Sequences*, 15. https://cs.uwaterloo.ca/journals/JIS/VOL15/Caldwell2/cald6.pdf (accessed 30 April 2016).

Chang, K. (2016) 'New biggest prime number', *New York Times*, www.nytimes.com/2016/01/22/science/
  new-biggest-prime-number-mersenne-primes.html (accessed 30 April 2016).
Thompson, I. (1995a) 'Count it out', *Child Education*, 72, 4: 18-19.
Thompson, I. (1995b) 'Out for the count', *Child Education*, 72, 3: 20-21.

Part II
Preventing, addressing and identifying children's errors

2 Statistics

In 1749 Gottfried Achenwall introduced the term *statistisch*, a word he derived from the Latin *statisticum*, in order to succinctly describe the collection and analysis of data pertaining to the state. As *statisticum* and other members of this word family, for example statista/statesman, were used by Latin speaking authorities to describe that which concerns the state I can see no logic which should have prevented Achenwall from doing so. Yet it was only a matter of time before John Sinclair would arrive on the scene, half a century later in 19th century Scotland to be precise, and use the term statistics to mean the general collection and evaluation of data that we know today. Ground breaking no doubt but when you consider Sir John of Ulbster wrote a total of 21 volumes in his 'Statistical Account of Scotland' it's surprising he didn't coin many more vernacular gems in this most prestigious of works. Though when you consider he was a politician who enjoyed writing about finance and agriculture on the side it's surprising he had time to sleep and we should be grateful he lasted long enough to give us this extremely succinct, useful and mathematical of terms.

Indeed, without Sir John of Ulbster 2014 would have been a very different place altogether. You see, for the first time, what had been known for generations as data handling or handling data depending on the publication - the general analysis and evaluation (handling) of miscellaneous data (data) - regained its true crown and the lineage was restored. I often imagine Achenwall and Sinclair tumbling off a certain waterfall in the Bernese Oberland region of Switzerland, the former insistent that only an analysis of the state can truly be defined by statistics, while the latter plummets safe in the knowledge that one day, yes one day those responsible for mathematics education will see the error of their ways and correct this most heinous of blunders. This etymological turpitude will be remedied!

Vocabularic precision

I soon realised, however, that it is irrelevant what it has come to be known as and as long as you are precise in your exploration of the inherent vocabulary then the more grandiose nature afforded by the title statistics should matter very little in reality. A point highlighted by my rather fanciful, though accurate I'm assured, account of its etymology. For those in the primary classroom (where it really matters for us) in England, statistics is a content area introduced in the 2014 English National Curriculum for the very first time in Year 2. It doesn't feature at all in Year 1 which is a complete shift from the previous incarnation of the National

Curriculum where you were expected to answer questions by recording information in lists and tables; present outcomes using practical resources and sorting objects into groups.

The noun itself, statistic, has come to mean a fact or piece of data obtained from a large quantity of numerical data, though rather ominously it could also signify an event or person regarded as no more than a piece of data. Let's hope they were going for grandiose rather than the significantly more derogatory inflection of the last description as there's enough difficulty in raising the profile of a sound understanding of shape without letting the value of statistics drop too. We need to keep all of those plates spinning regardless of the attention, prominence, status or importance given to them by Whitehall. There is nothing to say that this is the case and I truly believe the name change is intended to enhance the reputation of this particular content area rather than cause any slight or derogation. The impact of this, however, is a long way from being measured.

Collecting and representing data

On the surface it appears to be a literal collection and subsequent interpretation of data through the construction of relevant charts but there are many pitfalls to avoid. When pupils are asked to *interpret and construct simple pictograms, tally charts, block diagrams and simple tables* they must be made fully aware of the nature of each chart and the accuracies demanded to ensure equilibrium in the mathematical universe.

A typical pictogram

A typical pictogram will have x and y axes and will use pictures or photographs to represent a set amount of data. For example when measuring the number of children with different shoe sizes the y axis would be used to measure the quantity of pupils with each shoe size. Depending on the size of the sample this will vary from pictogram to pictogram. Subsequently the x axis will be used to denote several of the different shoe sizes. Again this will depend on the sample taken but in a typical class you may find a range such as size 12, size 13 and size 1 shoes. A picture of a shoe may be used to represent four children but it can easily represent any number you wish. With the benefit of such a graph being the ability to represent large amounts of data succinctly it makes sense that you choose a value greater than one for your picture or photograph. If we take a picture to represent a given value then it makes mathematical sense that half of that picture will represent half the set value. This can be easily stretched to represent a quarter of the original value but beyond this few benefits are to be found as the relative size of the picture can become difficult to determine.

Scales

When creating a pictogram we must be clear to ensure the pupils understand that the picture represents a given total, a multiple of 2, 5 or 10 at this stage, and that it is not merely a case of adding the pictures to garner a total. Always insist that the pupils are applying the skills learned from the statutory guidance on number. Insist that they count, add and even multiply in some cases. The pictogram is a valuable tool for representing larger amounts of data in a clear and concise manner so ensure your pupils know that it represents something much greater than the first glance intimates. This is a trap that children frequently fall into which can be so easily avoided if we ensure clarity of instruction and presentation.

Pictographs were used as one of the, if not the, earliest known forms of writing, and examples discovered in Egypt and Mesopotamia have been dated earlier than 3000 BCE, which causes me to draw the conclusion that our brains are hardwired to understand such visual representations and, if they aren't, we've had plenty of practice as a species over the last few millennia.

A typical tally

Usually tally charts are comprised of a series of horizontal lines where one horizontal line represents one. The values are usually collected in groups of five where four vertical lines crossed by one horizontal line represents the five and can be easily identified when counting the total of the tally. Pupils are thus able to apply their knowledge of the multiples of five rather than counting each horizontal line individually which can clearly become a cumbersome, monotonous and self-defeating process if the sample of the tally is large enough.

Cross-curricular links

In terms of cross-curricular links they don't come much easier than this. Egyptian civilisation is frequently covered over a six-week period in many primary schools and lo and behold they just happened to use pictographs to communicate. I insist that you take this opportunity to cover this particular statutory requirement via the time allotted for 'Egyptian Studies' rather than that which you designate for mathematical instruction. Obviously what you call these opportunities for learning will vary from school to school but there are many more mathematical concepts which will require a more discrete mode of delivery and you must grasp all fully formed links between content, regardless of the nature, with both hands for they come across with such ease much less than one would hope.

Tally charts are straightforward, pupils must know that a tally is a running total of results recorded during a survey and that its function is to serve as a crude representation of data collection. At this stage it is important to teach the children how they can collect the tallied results in the aforementioned bundles of five. This is done because it is considerably more efficient to count multiples of than individual marks when data is being analysed. Emphasise this with analysis of overly large numbers to show how mundane and futile it would be to try to collect an accurate total without making the smallest of errors and take the chance to reinforce how important it is to know the multiplication facts for the five times table. Just because the marks aren't Egyptian, Persian, Babylonian or Chinese in style doesn't mean they can't feature again in whatever particular area you have chosen to study as your overarching topic. Pictograms and tally charts go hand in hand, are vital when we conduct studies at the highest level and should be treated as a doorway to deeper learning, secure understanding and the most efficient working methods.

Blocks or bars

Block diagrams herald signs of things to come in the mathematics classroom, in my mind it's the precursor of the bar chart, and as such we must consider the common features of the mathematical understanding inherent in each concept. When representing continuous data such as distance, speed or time we must ensure the bars are touching so that the continuous nature of the data is represented accurately. When discussing with pupils it is worth saying that continuous data, and line graphs in particular, measure how something changes over time and as such we are looking to see a continuity in the data represented by a continuity in the visual representation.

Similarly, and likely much more relevant to younger pupils, when representing data that is not continuous we must ensure the bars *do not touch*. For them to touch would signify a continuous nature they simply do not have. Instead we search for a comparison between totals in the data and this acts as the basis of our analysis of discrete data. For instance when collecting data on shoe size, hair and eye colour, favourite film, favourite food, all of the stalwart infant data collections, we cannot suggest that size 5 and size 4 shoe sizes are continuous, they are entirely discrete and as such the bars *do not* (should not) *touch*. If there is but one thing you offer to your pupils in the way of statistical knowledge it should be this golden nugget of conceptual understanding. With continuous data the bars are continuous and with discrete data the bars are not continuous. Consider the implications this will have on your pupils over time as they move towards a complex interpretation and presentation of the world around them through statistical analysis and you will see that it is essential this point is presented as clearly and frequently as possible until the understanding is relational and the execution, of the pupils, fluent.

A quick online search will allow anyone to see how one could provide pupils with the opportunity for greater depth of learning and for the application of statistical understanding to increasingly abstract contexts. Using the resources available at www.nrich.maths.org for instance, classroom practitioners are able to broaden the mathematical experience on offer for pupils in relation to specific statistical objectives. You will see here that pupils are asked to reason, given open ended enquiries to participate in and that the opportunity to review solutions, and even provide their own solutions for others, something which is available for every problem and investigation on the website.

The list of examples you'll find in and throughout this book is not exhaustive but is certainly a good place to begin in your quest to challenge appropriately and broaden the maths curriculum you offer. In the past we may have accelerated pupils through interpretation towards the Year 5 and 6 objectives but now it is essential this type of deepening takes place to ensure our pupils are ready for the rigour of the Key Stage 3 and Key Stage 4 curricula.

One of the easiest traps to fall into when involved in statistical analysis in Year 2 involves the provision of suitable depth of analysis. Often we see questions akin to *how many people like cheese on toast, how many children had size five shoes,* and while they serve a purpose, they are the tip of the iceberg when it comes to pupil understanding. To teach a child to *ask and answer simple questions by counting the number of objects in each category and sorting the categories by quantity* is to provide them with examples of such questions, model the answer process and then provide opportunity to rehearse in a range of practical contexts.

Suitable challenge

In terms of providing opportunities for deeper understanding or practical application I would recommend the use of an investigation that not only increases the abstract nature of the problem to be solved at the appropriate level but is also suitably practical and engaging for younger pupils. The paragraph below explains one such problem quite succinctly and is an excellent example, in my humble opinion, of how we can prepare our pupils for future application, developing skills such as a systematic method of working which will be vital for the rest of the academic careers and beyond.

Drawing the axes of a graph on relatively large paper, perhaps even as big as that you would find on a flip chart, provide pupils with a resource which is both similar and different at the same time. Confusing perhaps but the main reason the resource I have come to know as 'compare bears' exists, largely because they are all bears but they are all different, usually colour, in some crucial way. For those who have not come across the term compare bears before, I simply refer to the collective term given to small plastic bears, identical except for size and colour, which are used to provide opportunity for children to draw comparisons based on the aforementioned differences. They are often found in packs of 30 which allows for a range of sorting activities to take place and, subsequently, a variety of abstract mathematical concepts to be presented in a concrete form.

Physically sorting the bears by colour on the axes and making a 3-D graph of sorts and asking challenging questions about the make-up of the graph allow you to extend pupils' understanding as outlined above. This can then link to the actual creation of graphs during which the skills can be drawn out for accurate graph making. Depending on the resource it may then be possible for pupils to create their own 3-D graph based on how they believe the resources can be sorted.

For a true extension you will then want the pupils to sort themselves, perhaps photographs could be used to place on the graphs, or name tags, it matters little as long as there is a representation for the pupils to manipulate. The discussion may then cover how they have been sorted, alternatives and the capturing of these graphs before the creation of accurate graphs in their books.

As this theme will run throughout the book, I urge you to remember that the example given is only one of many available and any planning session would not be complete without a reference to the array of resources where investigations can be found which you can tailor to the specific needs of your pupils. Like any resource we have access to it is worth considering the value as they stand and the value they hold as an idea or concept. You may choose to alter the investigation so that it takes on a greater role in your cross-curricular offering, create greater rigour or ease some of the cognitive burdens on your pupils, wholly dependent on their particular developmental level.

Resources

In my own practice I find that while I don't follow the large schemes and text books to the letter they are useful as a bank of ideas and examples of how learning can be fostered. I believe online resources can be treated in the same way and would implore you to adopt the practice of referring to relevant chapters or pages and considering the activities they suggest. Ask yourself if you can generate the required learning and if not do they form a starting point for something you can mould into an appropriate resource. The generation of activities which support the learning you want to encourage can be a difficult skill for those entering the profession or at the beginning of their careers and this is one of my top recommendations for new colleagues. As Roger Cole (2006) so adeptly points out 'too much freedom – chaos can ensue. Too much control – creativity can be stifled.' This rings as true for pupils as it does for teachers. Have this in the back of your mind always and use it to garner the perfect conditions for creativity in both you and your pupils.

As I will say at frequent milestones throughout this book, just because resources were created with a different curriculum or framework in mind doesn't mean they lose all of their value once the particular curriculum is replaced by another. Mathematics is a field of perpetual change but the rate at which this is happening is not so rapid that many of the generally accepted truths in 1998 are now defunct or negated. As such we can rest assured that much, if not all, of what we teach will remain accurate throughout the majority of our careers.

Comparing categorical data

Reflecting only on the expectations of the previous National Curriculum, the questions we expect pupils to ask can limit their progress and depth of understanding unless the opportunity to delve deeper is on offer. This is why I am pleased to see the inclusion of *totalling and comparing categorical data* in the statutory requirements. This is an addition which will allow pupils to explore the difference between categories and to understand the nature of analysis at a younger age. Pupils should now be encouraged to ask questions like *how much more rain fell in September than October?* and *how many people took part altogether?* In this way they can be introduced to the need and purpose of statistical analysis and to the very beginnings of looking for reliability within given data. *Can we trust this data? Is the sample large enough?* True analysis which can be drawn from such humble beginnings is important when trying to foster lifelong curiosity and desirable behaviours for learning. Considering we are expecting to see pupils of 6, 7 and 8 years of age developing skills which will be applicable when they are 26, 27, 28 years of age and beyond, this can only be a positive step in my book.

It is worth noting that statistics at Year 4 is almost identical to statistics at Year 3 and by the time we reach Year 3 we've already had a year of refurbished content where the boundaries should have been established for the creation of accurate and mathematically meaningful graphs and charts. The difference, as outlined in the notes and guidance, relates to the use of a greater range of scales and the introduction of graphical representations which change over time. The principles are the same but you must be aware of the nuances so that you are challenging your pupils appropriately.

Legally or statutorily, however our obligations as teachers may be described, the major difference is the fact that Year 3 pupils must be using simple scales of 2, 5 and 10 units per cm. I would add the caveat that they must be using these scales *at the very least* and strongly recommend the application of their understanding of place value through the scales they read and create. There may be those who consider these skills separate and I have considered the possibility that I may be overcomplicating the learning, but of this there is only a slight chance. It is much more likely that by combing the understanding of number you are challenging the pupils to apply their knowledge across the curriculum which is the current definition of working at age expectations (though even when it wasn't it was the minimum I would expect from a pupil as the skill without application is almost entirely redundant). This will have the desired effect of allowing you to conserve curriculum time, enhance the depth of your offering and challenge the more able appropriately.

Scales

If we consider the fact that between Year 3 and Year 4 the type of graph will change but the requirement to use a given scale does not, it may be worth including multiples of 6, 7, 9, 25 and 1,000 in the scales we provide as examples and opportunities for practice and application. Granted we very rarely see these multiples in the real world but I would counter this by imploring you to ask your pupils to find out why. Is there a reason we don't use variations outside of multiples of 2, 5 and 10 (with greatest emphasis and frequency on the latter of these) rather than alternatives? Are there examples of alternative scales across cultures? The opportunities to consider the reasons why and the origins of our habits and preferences can be as open ended as you like and provide a low threshold/high ceiling challenge for all pupils to access, regardless of their developmental level.

Keeping the origins of *statistisch* in mind and considering the purest model of what we are trying to achieve here – *what I would argue could be considered the development of pupils who are fluent and creative in their statistical analysis* – we should approach how we teach pupils to *solve comparison, sum and difference problems using information presented in bar charts, pictograms, tables and other graphs* with great enthusiasm, affording it the respect and time it deserves. I consider it our duty to provide our pupils with examples of such problems, the chance to see a model of the thought/answer process and before the careful provision of opportunity to rehearse in a range of practical contexts. By Year 4 pupils should be answering how many more, how many fewer and whereas that would have been considered the addition of extra depth in Year 2 it soon becomes the minimum expectation for statistical analysis, and rightly so.

Sorting

One of the most challenging problems I use refers to the sorting of a variety of objects against given criteria. Assisted by diagrams, pupils must apply their understanding of the presentation of information and their problem solving strategies to successfully navigate the problem. In a group of five friends, each child needs a chocolate bar for each year they have been at school and they are convinced they need more than the fifteen available. Their teacher, however, knows that this will in fact suffice. The teacher's solution is given but then pupils are given the following instruction as they are challenged to find their own solution to the problem. They must use exactly fifteen and, if they choose to represent it as such, given parts of the Venn diagram must contain a given number of chocolate bars based on how many years they have been at school. I would recommend a three circled Venn diagram as the most mathematically efficient method of recording their calculations and eventual solution but that will depend on the development of the pupils' understanding.

To increase the challenge you may choose not to give the initial solution or to provide further scaffold you may use concrete material such as hoops and actual chocolate. It really depends on how well you know your children and how much of a challenge you want to provide for them in each particular instance. What you can be sure of is the fact that it links directly with the expectations of the 2014 National Curriculum and learning that has been identified globally as significant in the mathematical progression of primary aged children.

Problems of a similar ilk but with the option of an interactive interface are known as 'Venn Diagrams' and 'More Carroll Diagrams' can be found at www.nrich.maths.org. While they can both be presented on a computer screen or monitor, the option to print the supporting materials is available, but the most interesting aspect for me is that 'More Carroll Diagrams' provides the opportunity for pupils to complete the diagram with given numbers and to label a completed diagram with the relevant headings. This for me is a win-win situation as it encourages pupils to think in a more abstract manner while preparing them for the type of thinking necessary to access the higher order questions included in the standardised end of key stage tests. It really would be very irresponsible not to try to foster this level of problem solving through such engaging resources.

Sum and difference problems

As they develop the ability to *solve comparison, sum and difference problems using information presented in a line graph* our responsibilities remain largely the same with the additional consideration of the impact of the introduction of continuous data and the misconceptions that may arise as a result. Having read this chapter you will no doubt have done several things. You will have carefully constructed many of your lessons, or their initial plans at least, so that they are entirely mathematically accurate and pupils are provided with a model of understanding that is pure in its mathematical accuracy and takes account of the possible misconceptions pupils may have e.g. touching bars and the representation of continuous and discrete data. Yet simultaneously you will have had one eye on the prize and consider the impact of acting on misconceptions in primary mathematics and designed a scenario where the misconception is entirely intentional but of this only you are aware. Deviant but effective no doubt! In doing so you will have shrewdly considered misconceptions alluded to in this chapter, covered all the bases for statistical analysis as we now know it while identifying, preventing and addressing children's errors. For more in a maths lesson, one cannot ask.

Pie charts and line graphs

Building on the line graph progression in Year 5, pupils in Year 6 must be able to *interpret and construct pie charts and line graphs and use these to solve problems*. If they have developed the required knowledge base in relation to angles then they will have a base of knowledge on which to build their understanding of angles, 360 degrees being the full complement of a pie chart. From there it's a matter of applying knowledge of multiples, factors and percentages to these angles in order to create a fluent expression of mathematical synaesthesia. If I have learned anything from my work in primary schools it is that a sound understanding and fluent use of multiples and factors is key to success in mathematics and in the introduction of the pie chart we see the coming together of many key skills, without which pupils will not be able to read and create pie charts to the required standard.

A pupil who is able to create an accurate pie chart is able to understand the concept of fractions and their equivalency with decimals and percentages, they are able to use effective written methods of mental division and multiplication; as previously stated they are aware of the fundamental importance of their multiplication and division facts, apply this knowledge on a scale of 10 and sometimes 100 times greater, and they are able to associate all this with the 360 degrees present in a circle. If they have a handle on all of this then pie charts are a piece of cake. Or pie as the case may be. I recommend you see this as an opportunity to use one content area to refine many skills. Where pupils are confused or you see misconceptions appearing they must ask themselves in which of these areas do they need further support, has a miscalculation led to an error, is there a gap in my knowledge I need to fill. If you are asking the same questions of each pupil as they assess their own conceptual understanding then you will be providing an environment in which a relational understanding can be grown.

Across the curriculum

A problem which I often set for pupils in groups of no less than two, such is the opportunity for meaningful discussion and debate, requires pupils to match sets of data to their respective headings. Depending on the overarching umbrella topic these headings could include anything from types of bird, species of animal or even those involved in a mystery of some sort. Though I must add you must be fully certain your pupils are mature enough to handle the context in which you choose to present the investigation and I would be wary of creating some sort of 'criminal' element without being 100% certain it is appropriate for your pupils.

I would typically give the pupils a range of charts and graphs, all dependent on their developmental level, that provide similar information and which can ultimately be read to deliver a conclusive outcome regarding that which they collegially describe.

Using only the information provided pupils must collaborate to identify and match the related data and headings. Only through the application of problem solving behaviours, suitable reasoning and an understanding of the data presented will the pupils be able to solve the problem. Simultaneously we are reinforcing their understanding of data handling and covering many bases at the same time; it is the essence of meaningful and relevant learning.

Timetables

I'm often amused, perhaps even bemused, when I see the National Curricula of the day explain that pupils must *complete, read and interpret information in tables, including timetables* (something which isn't very different from the old expectation at this point in the mathematics progression) as it stirs up visions of the unique melting pot we know as British society. In my mind practitioners are going to read this statutory requirement and react in two possible ways. If they live in an highly urban setting such as Inner London I assume they'll afford themselves the week off during maths lessons because the children in their class take two trains and the Circle Line on their way to school and have sussed the inner workings of a timetable with the military precision that can only be associated with exactly how long they have left before they really must get up.

The railway children

On the other side of the coin there will be practitioners entirely flabbergasted by how few children have actually ever seen a train before, let alone been a paying passenger on one. I insist that anyone in this situation, usually those who find themselves working in circumstances and catchment areas of high suburban socio-economic deprivation, immediately contacts the local train station and arranges for a full class expedition via train. Within this the opportunities for cross-curricular learning are phenomenal. You may sound the alarms and insist that you evacuate the children in a World War II-esque drill. The destination, a local town where the children will be distributed among the locals and made to work while they are kept safe from The Blitz. You may decide to double up on your list of things children must do and take them to the seaside, the theatre or a destination of local significance and value.

Meaningful application

Take them anywhere as long as the children are made aware that train journeys are both a means to an end and a pleasure in themselves. They must understand the history of the train, its importance to our society and how comparisons can be drawn with the ultramodern networks found in Asia and parts of Central Europe. They must be allowed to dream that one day all of our trains will be on time. This is an eventuality which will remove the necessity for many of our timetable skills but until that day comes insist that pupils are able to calculate their connections based on the late arrival of a train because as you know this is one of life's great certainties in modern Britain.

How you make timetable reading relevant to your pupils is by-the-by and there are some examples above but please do not create the situation where pupils are shown a timetable, told how to read it and then answer questions about it. Life is much richer than this and, where this particular content area is concerned, is where our priorities lie. Pupils must be allowed to analyse the appropriateness and effectiveness of timetables or information tables but without real life context this will not truly be possible and the more meaningful and relevant the tables, the greater the understanding fostered.

Averages

When teaching pupils about the mean as an average it must be linked with statistical analysis that has gone before or with its real life applications. Pupils must be taught that they need to add all of the values tallied together then divide by the number of values to find the mean average. This can be quite confusing if you are not clear so I would highly recommend identifying values, tally, total and modelling the process repeatedly to the pupils. Otherwise there is great potential for the development of misconceptions. As always there is a need to be precise in your description and modelling of the process and pupils must be aware of the relevance/impact this will have on their lives, both mathematical and 'real'. With averages I would always recommend breaking the concepts into smaller steps, introducing at the beginning of the year and returning to it through a variety of contexts so that interleaving can be used to develop understanding over a gradual period of time.

The mean is mentioned specifically in the 2014 National Curriculum but I believe pupils must be provided with a range of possible averages to calculate combined with an understanding of the context in which they can be used to ensure you aren't just teaching averages that might appear on the standardised tests but rather averages than can be encountered as a human being.

The mode is the most common value or the value that appears the most. I always emphasise the o sound in mode and most to provide pupils with a mnemonic type device to draw upon in the times of difficulty that will no doubt precede fluency. To calculate the mode put them in order and check which one appears the most.

Example: 2 5 5 3 9 12 12 14 5 becomes ...
            2 3 **5 5 5** 9 12 12 14 becomes ...
            5 is the mode

The *median* is the middle value. I emphasise the very slightly tenuous link between the sound of med and midd in middle again to try to provide the pupils with a mnemonic type device to draw upon in the times of difficulty that will no doubt precede fluency. However tenuous it may be. To calculate the median put them in order and find the number in the middle.

Example: 2 5 5 3 9 12 12 14 5 becomes ...
            2 3 5 5 **5** 9 12 12 14 becomes...
            5 is the median

Where there are two median values, in an example with an even number of values, the median is half way between the two.

Example: 2 5 5 3 9 12 12 14 6 7 becomes ...

2 3 5 5 **5 6** 9 12 12 14 becomes ...

5.5 is the median

The *range* is the difference between the biggest and smallest values so to calculate it you must put the numbers in order to find the biggest and smallest value then subtract.

Example: 2 5 5 3 9 12 12 14 6 7 becomes ...

2 3 5 5 **5 6** 9 12 12 14 becomes ...

14 - 2 = 12

The range is 12

The *mean* is found by dividing the total of the values by the number of values itself.

Example: 2 + 5 + 5 + 3 + 9 + 12 + 12 + 14 + 6 + 7 becomes ...

75 divide by 10 = 7.5

7.5 is the mean

This is the average pupils will need to statutorily be aware of so ensure their understanding is sound and that they are able to fluently calculate as such. Those who pursue a career in mathematics or the sciences will eventually come across a wider range of averages, no pun intended, such as the cubic, generalised or weighted means but for now it is sufficient that they understand that in the 16th century those astronomers who tried to measure the distance, speed or diameter of planets could only do so initially through the use of what we know today as the (arithmetic) mean.

Oh Little Town of Bethlehem

To enhance the depth of understanding I could suggest many possible investigations and problems but the one I would recommend as having the most scope for development provides pupils with two tables: this can be any information you choose, perhaps something relevant to the learning taking place across the curriculum, the Olympics are often popular during leap years, or perhaps the 'Roman Census' around Christmas time, even your own, confidentiality approved, version of the school census. When they have the data pupils are then required to analyse using their understanding of averages. This goes beyond a mere ability to calculate the average and really gives an importance or relevance to skill while challenging pupils at a deeper level. Ask the pupils to provide clear explanations of any trends they may have found, conclusions they can draw or anomalies they may have found.

If this is something that works well then you may want to access similar sports records or the Domesday Book which will provide further opportunity for true analysis of data and the development of key life skills.

Really, when you consider the origins of much of the content we have covered from the field of statistics, even at the primary level, there are several areas of learning with a deep and varied history which has resonated throughout the ages and acted as a societal cornerstone. Multiply this with the depth to which the concepts can be integrated into a broad and balanced curriculum and the value to the classroom practitioner becomes almost incalculable. It is a fool who does not consider the importance and the gravity of statistical analysis when considering the learning of the primary pupil and it is a greater fool who does not enrich the learning as is truly possible. This sentiment runs throughout the National Curriculum and throughout our understanding of our role in society. Take this opportunity to grab the bull by the horns, spin the plate and, most importantly, enrich the lives of the pupils in your care!

Reference

Cole, R. (2006) *The Creative Imperative: Unravel the Mystery of Creativity*. Lichfield: Primary First.

3 Algebra

I have no doubt the mere mention of the word algebra will strike fear in the heart of many so I'll tackle it head on relatively early. Really though there is very little to the algebra required in the National Curriculum, which incidentally only officially appears in the Year 6 requirements, so aside from ensuring your subject knowledge is up to speed there is really nothing to be concerned about.

Early sign posts

While in England we may say algebra only officially appears in Year 6 the keen eye, however, will notice the preparatory nature of recognising patterns, sequencing, conjecturing and generalising in Key Stage 1 alongside patterns and sequencing in Key Stage 2. The commutativity and associativity of addition, proper use of the equals sign, relations between quantities and the effect of adding and subtracting zero all feature heavily in the preceding pages of the National Curriculum and act as a pathway to the eventual introduction of formal algebraic notation and thinking. Without these skills, and the understanding inherent within them, pupils will struggle to access the formal notion of algebraic processes and notation so it is essential we identify the key steps along the way and make it explicit, or at least be aware yourself of where they are in the journey towards fluent use of formulae and problem solving.

Setting bones

Al-Ḵwārizmī (Algoritmi), a mathematician known for some notable contributions to mathematical terms across the globe, first used an etymological cousin of the word we know as algebra in his book *The Science of Restoring What Is Missing and Equating Like With Like*. Al-jabr, the Arabic term for setting bones, moved through Italy and Spain until it came to represent the study of mathematical symbols and concepts we know today and it is useful to bear this in mind when you consider your approach. Like for like – marrying that which has been separated, this is what they had in mind when they first described the concept many years ago.

Simple formulae

In Year 6 pupils *must use simple formulae*. Formulae is the plural of formula and a formula is a mathematical relationship or rule expressed in symbols. We are all no doubt familiar with Pythagorean theory but even that is overcomplicating things at this stage. Your pupils should know how to calculate the area and perimeter of a rectilinear shape and thus should be well prepared to describe the rule for such calculations: 2 (a + b) for perimeter, a = lw for area. Simple, straightforward and to the point. Once they see this you can then open up the possibility that they create their own description of the relationships and rules they encounter.

As far as an explanation of this goes, it is useful to have an image of a rectilinear shape to refer to; I recommend an oblong for increased clarity, when explaining the links between the abstract and the pictorial. With perimeter it is best to identify a and b first, a being the length of one side and b the width. Show the pupils a, point to it and tell them this is a, it is the length of one side and repeat with b. Ask the pupils if they notice anything about a and b and hopefully the conversation will come round to the fact that there are two of each in this particular rectangle. You may have a pupil realise that they will need to multiply by 2. At this point explain that there are rules for calculation whereby terms within brackets must be approached first and that it is only once you have added a + b that you can multiply by two. Refer also to the fact that the absence of an operation means you must multiply the terms beside each other. But more on this in a moment.

Formulae

In my own experience I find the best way to develop the use of formulae is to present pupils with representations of the shapes, perhaps with a and b labelled on some and actual lengths on others. I ask them to create a formula that explains how to calculate the perimeter of any shape and we refine as they come up with suggestions, explaining that we want the most succinct formula possible. You'll often find that they'll begin with a + a + b + b = p or something similar, depending on how you intervene they will then try a + b x 2 and so on until they are guided towards the actual formula. So it is very much a case of analysing each situation before deciding how you would choose to approach the refinement process.

Any exploration of the formula for calculating the area of a rectilinear shape should be approached in the same way. Representations are shown, some with letters, some with numbers, though it may not be necessary to have letters in this case as it could prove to be intuitive to use the relative notation. Certainly try to enable the pupils to generate as much as possible as it will only be a matter of time before you will need to get involved. For, you see, no input on this particular formula would be complete without discussion around the use of the letter x and its role as the operative symbol for multiplication. As the letter x can be both used in notation, as much as y, z or any other letter of the alphabet can be, and as the aforementioned multiplication symbol, there are two possible solutions to this problem.

$$\frac{6}{7-x}$$

Figure 3.1

As you can see from Figure 3.1 a slight variation of the letter x can be used so that it is drawn with curled ends so to speak when acting as the letter x. This in turn leaves the regular formation of the letter x to operate as a symbol. It is rare, however, to see this and as such the second, more frequent, solution is recommended.

In these instances the letter x is left to act as a letter in the notation of a formula and the absence of an operational symbol is used to command the multiplication of all in its path. This is where we find ourselves with the formula a = lw. It could be a = l × w representing area = length × width but I feel this is rather confusing and counterproductive. Make the link between the absence of an operation between the l and the w and you will overcome any possible misconceptions, should you follow the guidance.

I personally would encourage pupils to describe their encounters with formulae and patterns using algebra, or at least algebraic foundations, throughout their careers and move from the use of words to describe to the use of symbols to describe the formulae as their understanding progresses. Newton's second law of motion, or $\vec{F} = m\vec{a}$ to the classical physicists among you, is another great example you can make practical. Simply put, it says that the force on an object is equal to the mass x action (the action being the push you give to a ball for instance) and while pupils may not be able to work with this in real terms because they can't measure the push accurately enough, they can certainly be shown how the value of something can be described by a single letter. The non-statutory guidance suggests you cover formulae in mathematics and science so here we have two starting points on which you can build. Another fascinating example is e = mc^2 but as yet your children can't travel at speed c. 186,000 mph, and as such are unlikely to be able to test it out in their lifetimes.

Linear sequences

We have touched on the notion and precursory nature of objectives related to the *description of linear number sequences* in prior chapters, the beginnings of which can be seen in Year 2, and really we must consider how the expectations have evolved. Is it a case of more difficult numbers or could there be something more to it? This is one instance in which the statutory guidance is not so explicit or particularly supportive and while it does make reference to *the generalisation of number patterns* there isn't much else in the way of explanation. At this point I would consider using sequences as an opportunity to reflect on the skills learned in previous years and to develop sound working habits for the increasingly complex investigations at hand.

In this particular investigation pupils are presented with five sequences of numbers which they must complete by calculating the appropriate rule. Straightforward perhaps, but put children in pairs and support the dialogue where necessary and you will provide opportunities for meaningful reasoning and investigation.

This should then be linked to some of our more widely known number sequences, the Fibonacci sequence perhaps, triangular numbers and perhaps even Pascal's triangle. Each can be described through an algebraic formula and should be used as a link to the real life application of mathematics. Aside from forming the building blocks of life, Fibonacci's sequence can be used to enhance search engine algorithms, something which our pupils will no doubt be familiar with even if they don't yet understand the mechanics. In addition a combination of triangular numbers and Fibonacci's triangle is said to have benefits in the world of probability and gambling but there's a high probability you, and your employer, won't want to suggest that particular example to primary aged pupils.

My favourite investigation

When it comes to number sequences there are many investigations available which will develop the investigative, reasoning and collaborative skills of your pupils while simultaneously enhancing their understanding of particular sequences and the overarching concept of the sequence. My personal favourite introduction to algebraic number sequences involves the use of multi-link cubes, stacked vertically initially, and the number of faces on show. Using up to a maximum of 10 cubes pupils must systematically create a table recording the number of cubes, the number of faces visible without moving the tower and the difference between them. It is then up to pupils to formulate a rule for turning the number of cubes into the number of faces by asking them how do we calculate any number in the sequence e.g. 76th. Their initial response will be to say calculate them in order until they reach 76 cubes but I ask them to explain what we do to one to generate five that we also do to two to generate nine, three to thirteen and so on. I explain that it is only a rule if it applies in all instances.

At this point it is your role to support them when they make mistakes. Only the very able will be able to see the pattern immediately and it will generally take some trial and error before pupils will come to see the pattern. Once they do, however, it is up to them to explain their reasoning: how did they find the pattern and can they apply this understanding to a tower which is arranged horizontally?

Each of the examples has its own unique formula based on the number of faces we can see. In the first example we can always see four sides on each cube plus one face on top of the tower. We can't see the bottom face as it is hidden from view so each time we can see 4 faces +1. Algebraically you could say that n (the number of faces) is equal to (n4) +1 or the number of cubes multiplied by 4 +1 in words. As a formula I would record this (n4) + 1 though the brackets may not be entirely necessary. For me though they give a certainty to the pupils at primary level that the multiplication must happen first then the 1 should be added otherwise the figures will be skewed.

As you have probably worked out when the tower is presented horizontally three faces are visible on each cube, plus one at either end of the tower (see Figure 3.2). This means, in words, that the number of cubes can be multiplied by 3 each time and a further 2 added to take account of the ever visible faces at the end. In algebraic notation this could be written as (n3) + 2 where again the brackets are not necessarily essential but I feel they add clarity at this level of pupil understanding.

Cubes	Faces	Difference
1	5	4
2	9	7
3	13	10
4	17	13
5	21	16
6	25	19
7	29	22

Figure 3.2

Missing number problems

Once you've got that sorted and algebra has been thoroughly introduced it is of increasingly more use to understand how pupils should *express missing number problems algebraically*. Not least for the double dose of reasoning and problem solving Year 6 pupils will have to endure during standardised testing where this kind of skill will prove priceless for those trying to reach the highest level possible within the scaled scoring system.

This is also something which will provide evidence of a true understanding of the extremely abstract world of algebra and has been described succinctly by the example given in the curriculum $a + b = b + a$. The interchangeability of the letters should provide plenty of opportunity to explore the concept of missing numbers and if they understand the value attachments to letters as outlined earlier in this section then they will be able to access this without issue.

I would strongly recommend that you familiarise yourself with the plethora of resources available, many via social networking such as Twitter where there are a large number of mathematics groups focused on improving the quality of primary education, surrounding the application of algebra. A programme known as 'Mathematical Allsorts' is available through the ATM, the Association of Teachers of Mathematics, which provides a reasonable progression through the skills necessary to think and reason algebraically and fosters the behaviours and habits associated with effective mathematical investigation. All this without any mention of number, allowing all pupils to access the investigations at their level of reasoning and understanding which provides opportunity for suitable challenge and depth as they progress.

The National Centre for Excellence in the Teaching of Mathematics, or NCETM for short, is an excellent resource that I implore you to make the most of. You are required to register as a member but this actually has very little impact on your daily life if you choose to opt in and out of their resources. The site itself is easily navigated and I won't dare to talk specifics when it could make this publication out of date in the blink of an eye but when you identify the link to 'teaching resources' the number of links available to resources associated with 'algebra and pre-algebra' has reached a significant figure and is steadily rising.

Resources include fully planned workshops which can be delivered to members of your team or specially chosen groups of staff. The workshops I have found via the NCETM website each follow a similar pattern whereby an overview of the aims of the workshop is given alongside any resources, suggested activities and suggestions for further reading. Links to the relevant learning and skills are presented and a clear run through of the activities is available when you download a 'whole workshop' zip file. Even if you aren't head of department it may be worth casting your eye over particular areas of interest, weakness or importance in order that you can take responsibility for your own continued professional development in the truest sense of the word.

In the same offering there are support packs, links to articles or research of significance and the publications where they can be found, materials that will help prepare for high quality lessons and extension materials. Combine this with the fact that the site itself supports members in the development of online CPD, the creation of a learning journal, networking and the utilisation of a self-evaluation tool, it leaves me wondering how anyone in the profession is not yet registered and making the most of the wealth of opportunities and support on offer.

If a pupil is attaining the expected level then they will be prepared for the algebraic rigour of the National Curriculum but as you have seen they will also need the problem solving skills necessary to unpick at the appropriate depth as well. The non-statutory guidance identifies missing numbers, lengths, coordinates and angles as the key to using simple formulae and if pupils understand the processes through which they can unpick a formula, as outlined earlier, then they will be able to unpick the question and approach as is required.

I often hear people joke about how little they use what they learned at school and algebra usually features quite regularly in this entirely witless tradition. Similarly I hear people laugh and nonchalantly boast about how they were never very good at maths at school and how this has continued into the present day. No doubt a social abscess which must be treated sooner rather than later, I am shocked that in the 21st century grown adults can hold this position and not feel the deep sense of shame often felt by those who are illiterate. I've never heard anyone boast about how they never learned to read so why should it be socially acceptable to claim we don't know our times tables or never really understood algebra?

I have some expectation that this 'boasting' is the physical manifestation of potentially deep-set insecurities but regardless, it should not be acceptable in our society. For if it wasn't then those who have not sought to rectify the gaps in their knowledge would certainly do so post-haste. Little do they realise that beyond the mystic facade of letters and symbols, deep in the centre of algebra there lies a set of key skills which we can all benefit from in one way or another. To not apply the skills necessary to access algebra I can only assume is to exist in a vacuum devoid of all interaction with other human beings. When it comes time to provide your pupils with a deep and meaningful understanding of algebra be sure to give them a rounded picture where the content knowledge and the skills are held in equal esteem for then you may just have taken the first steps to eradicating a known scourge on society.

Rant over.

For the moment.

4 Number and place value

Having cut our teeth on statistics and algebra it is now time to get stuck into a content area which can, unsurprisingly you might say, account for up to 80% of our focus as classroom teachers. And while this may be a disproportionate representation when correlated against the breadth of primary mathematics, there may be method in our madness/bias. You see, if pupils are to attain the standard expected of them and highlighted in the aims of the 2014 National Curriculum, whereby they are fluent in the fundamentals of mathematics, can reason mathematically and solve problems involving the application of their mathematics in a variety of routine and non-routine problems, then they will need to have a relational understanding in the building blocks of mathematics.

For me the concepts we meet in number and place value form the foundations for everything else pupils will encounter in primary mathematics and beyond. If a pupil can't apply their knowledge of decimal place value then what hope do they have of converting between fractions and percentages? If they don't understand the relative size of numbers then how do they hope to interpret graph scales or decode the place value of the numbers engraved on the side of their measuring cylinders or weighing scales? Most importantly, if they cannot read Roman numerals then how can we ever expect them to learn to tell the time at their nan's house?

Well, perhaps not the last one but you should get the point. Everything we meet in number will keep us in good stead across the rest of the mathematics curriculum and make it that bit easier to navigate. I believe this is the main reason why the standardised tests are so heavily weighted in favour of number, and problem solving as of May 2016, because the importance of a relational understanding in this key content area cannot be overstated. While we progress through our academic careers and into the world of work there is a strong likelihood any mathematics we do apply will be grounded in number and the building blocks covered at a primary level, particularly as primary level mathematics in 2016 morphs into something more akin to GCSE mathematics circa 2005. Therefore, as we move towards a full and proper consideration of number and place value I merely ask that you keep the importance and weighting of this particular content area at the forefront of your mind during your delivery of primary mathematics.

Counting

Initially, pupils in Year 1 should be taught to *count to and across 100, forwards and backwards, beginning with 0 or 1, or from any given number.* This can be taught without any formal lesson structure and introduced through daily counting using the counting stick. The opportunity to count shouldn't be exclusive to Key Stage 1 but it must certainly be ever present in the formative years of number conservation. Utilising the stick can provide opportunity to count to and across 100, forwards and backwards, beginning with any number of your choosing. Everything mentioned in this particular statutory requirement. When setting out the counting ground rules it is important to insist that pupils respect the following rules:

- The stick is a visual representation, it links the images of the left brain and the numbers of the right – you must visualise when counting.
- Only say the number when I touch the division – rhyming off a list of numbers is not the intended outcome.
- Count clearly and confidently when you are asked to – respect others when you are not.
- I will try and catch you out by jumping from number to number.
- Be prepared to explain your thinking at any moment (*particularly when exploring factors, multiples and properties of a number, which will become more pertinent as children grow older and counting becomes more complex*).

From here it is a matter of modelling the expected behaviours when counting, planning sufficient challenge for your pupils and providing opportunity to count and to improve this most vital of skills on a daily basis. As you will see from the links that can be drawn between counting and multiplication/division those children who do count for 15 minutes a day are those who will make the most rapid and sustained progress. The teacher who does not provide ample opportunity starves their pupils of the oxygen necessary to grow and loses the advantageous nature of incorporating whole statutory requirements into daily counting sessions rather than using valuable teaching time.

Through the use of the counting stick, our youngest pupils must be taught to *count, read and write numbers to 100 in numerals; count in multiples of twos, fives and tens* and this is where we can see the introduction of the difference between recitation and enumeration. The counting stick can be used to explore multiples but we must balance this with the opportunity to read and write numbers to 100 in numerals. Whatever medium pupils encounter the numbers in you must use the term numeral to describe the written form of the numbers. The numbers are represented in numerals, the number fourteen being represented by the numerals 1 and 4. This attributes no value to the digits but is merely an accurate description of the constitution the pupils see before them. We don't say 'What number do we draw first when we write 14?' rather we should say 'What numeral should we record first when writing the number 14?'

Deepening understanding

With the aim of extending the depth at which pupils are counting you may wish to consider the use of playing cards, coins or dominoes as a way of allowing pupils to build sequences of numbers and explore the use of abstract representation of numbers in a given sequence. This can be differentiated to meet the needs of any particular group at the relevant developmental level but in the example given here I would suggest that pupils are encouraged to use a given medium to represent the counting that has taken place, for instance, in a preceding counting stick session. You may ask them to use playing cards to show the sequence of multiples of 2 from 2 to 20. With this in mind pupils would need to decide how they represent the numbers from 12 onwards. Would they naturally gravitate towards the use of the Queen to represent 12, would the Ace represent 14 and would 16 then become a Queen and a Two, 18 a Queen and a Four or an Ace and a Two, and so on? Or can they provide an alternative and equally valid solution? There isn't just one answer and it can apply to denominations of coin or any other given method of representation, whereby various combinations are used to represent the given numbers and then affixed to the counting stick as an abstract aid to counting. How you tweak this investigation is entirely down to the developmental level of your pupils and I feel even taking such an approach is a step towards fostering greater fluency in your pupils.

And while the expectation *steps of 2, 3, and 5 from 0, and in tens from any number, forward and backward* forms a natural progression from the Year 1 expectations we should see little difference in how this should be taught and the skills/procedural knowledge involved. In fact this applies whether we set the expectation of *counting in multiples of 4, 8, and 50 from 100*, a natural, if not ambitious, progression from Year 2 to Year 3, *counting in multiples of 6, 7, 9 and 25 and 1,000, counting forward or backwards in steps of powers of 10 for any given number up to 1,000,000* or *reading, writing, ordering and comparing numbers up to 10,000,000 and determining the value of each digit*, by which time they will have a fluent command of place value and will already be making moves towards a mathematics devoid of numbers entirely.

The foundations built through counting should run consistently throughout your school and it should be embraced as a force for the good and strategy we can rely on to enhance pupil achievement. Pupils should count every day and practitioners should link this counting to any objectives where possible. Pupils who do not know their multiplication tables and do not understand the concept of counting in multiples are at a significant disadvantage to their peers and you should treat this as an ongoing priority. Recitation and enumeration as habitual practices should have been established throughout the mathematical careers of your pupils and if they have been established correctly they will have put your pupils in good stead for the learning you expect to take place during your time with them and beyond.

Depth is key

When I first began working with the expectations of the 2014 National Curriculum, where greater depth is encouraged in place of acceleration through the objectives, I came across the use of binary as a tool to promote a deeper understanding of the place value. Where our pupils are used to working in base 10 and decimalisation we can only truly test their understanding of the core principles if we provide them with opportunity to work in a different base, base 2 in this case. As binary has some relevance to the computing world, though considerably less than it once did, and is used primarily in the development of computer apps I feel it is the best alternative to base 10 for our pupils to explore.

Once a brief explanation of the binary system, whereby only two digits are used in the representation of all numbers and the units of measurement double in size each time – 1, 2, 4, 8, 16, 32, 64, 128, etc. – has taken place, I would provide pupils with a blank hundred square, perhaps with the first five numbers in place, and ask them to complete it. If they truly understand the concepts inherent in base 10 then they will, or should, be able to apply them to base 2. If this is the case, and pupils can successfully manipulate the 1s and 0s to the point of a complete binary hundred square I would then suggest they are provided with the computing opportunities to apply this knowledge and understanding. Something I have every expectation is a key aspect of the computing curriculum, and if it isn't will surely be relevant to lives they will one day lead in the world of work.

I would highly recommend that even if they have had a diet which has been rich and varied and offered opportunity to count and form models and images that you continue to use the counting stick to reinforce the concepts, patterns and habits which have been forming over time. If your pupils, or even a set few, have not had such a diet then it is extremely important you provide the opportunities as quickly and as frequently as possible. Follow the guiding principles, be consistent and you will see dramatic improvements in the understanding and fluency of your pupils.

Recitation and enumeration

If nothing else the 2014 National Curriculum reminds us of the importance of the establishment of recitation and enumeration as habitual practices, occurring little and often so as to free the working memory for problem solving and other such trivial pursuits. And it is at this point I feel it most appropriate to explain that the counting stick can be used when working with negative numbers.

This can be done in two ways. You can alter the position of zero, always a good idea anyway when searching for fluency, or you can display the stick vertically instead of horizontally. This way it can represent a thermometer and use the context pupils will be most familiar with for negative numbers to enhance their understanding and provide suitable visual representation. You should also introduce the addition and subtraction of negative numbers so that pupils begin to formulate the representation. Again I would like to refer to the example given earlier which directed you towards the plethora of relevant material available online from video sharing sites such as YouTube and the archived materials related to the 1999 National Curriculum. Of course they may not refer directly to the objectives and requirements mentioned in this text but they can be extremely useful in developing techniques and strategies applicable in the modern classroom. Familiarise yourself with these materials and you will be able to take what is of use to the betterment of your practice and the understanding of the pupils in your care. Be warned, however, that any online reference to twelve count stick striking drills will in fact show a man with a stick and, to the best of my knowledge, is not an example of best practice.

Negative numbers

Negative numbers and their use is a concept that can often mislead pupils and misconceptions can form quite early on. Show them the patterns, how the numerals increase as the number decreases, how the numerals decrease as the number increases and the ever intricate workings of addition and subtraction. To cover all the possible variations outline clearly that two like signs become a positive sign and two unlike signs become a negative sign. For example $4 + (+5) = 4 + 5 = 9$ or $5 - (-2) = 5 + 2 = 7$, both the signs are alike and so a positive outcome is necessary. Similarly, $5 + (-4) = 5 - 4 = 1$ or $5 - (+2) = 5 - 2 = 3$, both the signs are different and we must use a negative sign to balance and complete the calculation. Mass panic, hysteria and a lifetime of confusion can follow if this subject isn't tackled head on and tackled accurately and efficiently. Pupils need to be clear in their understanding, you must explain why this is the case and how it came to be and although you may say that you feel this a little out of your remit we're in the 21st century and nothing is beyond the powers of the primary mathematics teacher.

Key to mastery

Truthfully we just need to consider the use of the number line as a visual representation of the value and properties of negative and positive numbers. Highlight how they interact with each other through appropriate models and images and the pupils, as always, will be able to move from the pictorial to the abstract with increased fluency. In terms of context it is always beneficial to use any impact temperature can have on scientific investigations in pharmaceutical companies, where I'm informed a lot of high temperature burning takes place and perhaps there may be avenues to explore in terms of the application of negative numbers. Though I would never recommend high temperature burning without the appropriate risk assessment and the presence of someone who knew what they were doing.

Equally it may be possible to use banking and stock trading as examples of the proficient use of negative numbers and the opportunities to calculate with these values appear limitless to me. In Year 5 the statutory requirements identify the need to *interpret negative numbers in context, count forwards and backwards with positive and negative whole numbers, including through zero.* I'm not entirely convinced this is asking any more than the relevant requirement in Year 4 but the principles of counting with negative numbers remain the same which, it must be said, is true of the Year 6 statutory requirements where they identify the need to *use negative numbers in context, and calculate intervals across zero.* So why not link it with something which impacts on our daily lives in a huge way yet few people actually understand? If we are talking about impact on understanding of the world in which we live a comprehension of exactly what bankers are up to and how 'The City' and Wall Street actually work would be right up there on my list of most valuable experiences and pools of knowledge.

Worthwhile perhaps, is the consideration of games where pupils try to reach one end of a given number line, for instance between -20 and 20, and as they roll dice or spin spinners pupils are able to move a given counter in a given direction by the number rolled or spun. For example Player 1 and Player 2 want to play this game. Player 1 aims to move the counter, which begins at 0 or the middle of the board, to -20. Their opponent, Player 2, aims to move the counter to 20. Each rolls or spins in turn and in the first move Player 1 spins a 3, they can move from 0 to -3, Player 2 rolls a 6 and they can move to 3, and so on until one of the players gets the counter to their assigned number. The difficulty can be increased by placing greater restrictions on ease of move or enforcing calculations prior to the move, for instance, only if the number you will land on is a factor of 2.

As you progress through your career I have no doubt you will often find one of the more popular objectives from any given National Curriculum is that, *given a number,* pupils will be able to *identify one more and one less.* Here the counting stick's visualisation, which we are constantly making reference to, will be of great use, as will the rich diet of opportunity provided within your counting planning. Yet for me, the most important aspect of this particular requirement is that too much time is not spent where it is not necessary. This is often a popular objective with parents because they have access to the means by which they can teach this procedural knowledge at home. If this is the case then this should not become their main target. Yes it is key but only where it is not present in pupils' understanding already. Every opportunity should be taken to deepen the understanding of pupils who can identify one more and one less from any given number. It may be wise to consider the type of question you are asking to these pupils.

Questioning

Does your questioning provide opportunity for deeper understanding or a stretch to the next, metaphorical, level? If not, you should consider the openings of the question. A slight tweak can make all the difference to a pupil's progress. You may want to develop the level of thought and reason they have injected into the process. Perhaps you could ask them how they know, why this is the case, if their solution is the best solution, are there any patterns, what might happen next or if any comparisons can be drawn. That is not to say that every child will be ready to comprehend such enquiries, many will need to be taught, but the earlier you start the greater their fluency as they grow and perfect their skills. This is a prime example of how a simple, procedural, requirement can be taken to a new level through the introduction of questioning techniques. All I ask is that you consider the challenge available to your pupils each and every day.

The inclusion of pupils *finding 1,000 more or less than a given number* is really an opportunity for them to show their fluency and confidence with the patterns in the base 10 system and, realistically, is no more related to 1 more and 1 less than the man on the moon but they do share some key properties. Pupils should be taught, where necessary, to identify the key digits and manipulate them, as you would with 1 more and 1 less, while always having one eye on the place holders in use. Eventually they will be expected to alter numbers by any give power of 10 and this forms the beginnings of that progression. To find 1,000 more or less is to alter the units in 10 to the power of 3 or 10x10x10. This means the 1,000 column will change. Draw attention to this fact, use this language and you will do well to prepare them for the next step in the progression.

When teaching pupils to *identify and represent numbers using objects and pictorial representations including the number line* there isn't much that hasn't already been covered in this counting section, suffice to say that once again a richness in the language used and opportunity provided should be your top priority. I find it interesting and reassuring that specific mention is given at this point to teaching pupils the language of *equal to, more than, less than (fewer), most and least*. The fact that they are statutory requirements at the time of writing matters little in comparison with their importance in the development of a bank of language which can be applied to the description and comparison of number. Give priority in your own mind to the use of this vocabulary, write it on your planning, give the terms and their meaning prominence in the classroom, do anything which will remind you of the key, and statutory, vocabulary you must embed in the minds of your pupils and eventually it will become second nature.

The number line – friend or foe?

The introduction of the number line is an interesting proposition given the interest the Department for Education had in China, Shanghai in particular, around the time the 2014 National Curriculum was finalised and introduced. Interesting in as much as those pupils and teachers I spoke to had no idea why anyone would want to use a number line, let alone a blank number line for that matter. It is a progressive step they must choose to omit and while this may be anecdotal evidence it is evidence nonetheless of an alternative view to the one proposed by both the National Curriculum and myself. Pupils are expected to *identify, represent and estimate numbers using different representations, including the number line* which for me suggests the use of the number line, in conjunction with apparatus such as Dienes equipment as a tool for creating concrete representations of abstract numbers or calculations.

Certainly when a blank or empty number line is used to calculate we often begin with the largest number and partition the other number accordingly as shown in Figure 4.1. At this point no calculation is expected but it almost certainly will be when it comes to addition and subtraction so make sure your pupils are familiar with a range of representations and the composition of each 2-digit number. This will be something they become familiar with as they make their way towards an understanding of numbers to 10,000,000 and beyond.

Eventually, as you travel through the progression, there is no reference to the number line when pupils are expected to *identify, represent and estimate numbers using different representations,* which for me suggests the use of apparatus such as Dienes equipment as a tool for creating concrete representations of abstract numbers or calculations. A total understanding of the number should now manifest itself as partitioning numbers in a variety of ways, e.g. 255 and 200, 50 and 5 or 250 and 5 or 210 and 45, allows the pupils to show a degree of control not expected before when working with numbers. Naturally as the expectation on the size of the number grows so too will the partitioning and this example must be recognised as only one possible connotation which doesn't take into account 4, 5, 6 or 7 digit numbers. Non-statutory guidance suggests that it is also an opportunity for

55 + 13

55_____65_____68
                (+10)   (+3)

Figure 4.1

links to be made with measure so that representations are seen in a variety of ways to ensure they can apply to real life. One of the key reasons for any mathematical learning.

If all of the aforementioned learning, relevant to year group of course, is taken into account then by the time your pupils leave Year 1 they should be able to *read and write numbers from 1 to 20 in numerals and words*. In fact, I would be surprised if they weren't already beginning to manipulate the quantities of objects and experimenting with the abstract concept of number conservation in a more formal and direct way. Then by the time your pupils leave Year 2 they should be able to *read and write numbers to at least 100 in numerals and words,* experimenting with the abstract concept of number conservation in a more formal and direct way, if not having begun to understand the value of zero as a place holder. Continuing on, when your pupils leave Year 3 they should be able to *read and write numbers to at least 1,000 in numerals and words* and while I would never recommend teaching to the test, there is an expectation that by the end of Key Stage 2 pupils will be able to write numbers in words accurately so it would be a disservice not to provide opportunity, perhaps when practising letter formation, to record them in this way with increased frequency and accuracy.

Strangely perhaps, there is no mention of this in the Year 4 curriculum but you should continue to insist that the correct spelling is non-negotiable and provide opportunities for those with gaps to practise. Remember the end of Key Stage 2 expectation and your commitment to provide sufficient opportunity for your pupils to not only achieve the expected standard but to ensure their mathematical diet is so rich that they have no choice but to succeed and continue on this path long past their academic careers.

You may wish to challenge your more able pupils, regardless of year group, to develop their own system of representation, such as base 10, for the mathematics they encounter when learning about number and place value. You may be surprised at what they come up with and certainly you will have provided opportunity for them to consider what the core principles of what they are learning really are. Children are often keen to create their own lessons and this is an example of where you could give them an objective and ask them to plan how they would teach children in the preceding year about the particular concept. There is something to be said about the notion that you only truly understand something when you can teach it so there may be something in our expectation that pupils sometimes take responsibility for the learning of others as well.

In terms of mathematical understanding it is essential you maintain the clarity of instruction when using terms such as number, numeral, counting and digit. If there is any confusion at this point it could potentially have a lasting effect on the conceptual understanding of your pupils. It is worth taking the time to ensure they understand exactly what it is you mean when you use mathematical terms and that they begin to assimilate the correct usage as early as possible. This, I feel, will have an impact on their understanding and reasoning when they can use the vocabulary you began using at an early age.

Know your definitions

If nothing else, remember that a numeral is a symbol or name that stands to represent a number, which in turn is an arithmetical value, expressed by a word, symbol or figure, representing a given quantity. 0–9 are the digits we use to form numbers and are not to be confused with the homophone which has come to mean finger, thumb or toe. When discussing the reading, writing, ordering and partitioning of numbers, to which we will come shortly, you could do much worse than to have these definitions up your sleeve and to encourage even the youngest of pupils to use them on a regular basis.

This in turn leads us on nicely to the expectation that pupils *recognise the place value of each digit in a two-digit number*. For they must now do so using the terms tens and ones, something which caused a furore I can assure you when primary teachers, particularly in Year 2 and Year 6, across the land realised this momentous continental shift. You see, prior to 2014 the broader education lexicon described the ones as units and all was well with the world until someone realised that actually the term units describes a unit of measurement, whatever size they may be, no matter the constitution.

The ones are a unit of measurement, the tens a unit of measurement and the hundreds a unit of measurement, which all coincidentally fall into the class of 'the hundreds'. The class is signified by how we read the numbers which fall into it, for example 143 is one hundred and forty three. Were the class to fall into the thousands we would make reference to how many thousands, millions, etc. with no end in sight, e.g. 143,609 is read as one hundred and forty three thousand, six hundred and nine. The classes are used to structure the oral recitation of the number, demarcated by a comma in the United Kingdom or a space, and sometimes even a decimal point (madness I know) in Central Europe. It may seem like a tangent but this is the very basis of the use of the term ones in the 2014 National Curriculum and as such it holds untold value to the understanding of a pivotal concept at primary level. As always, be very clear with your pupils as to the language, its usage and the reasons why. The earlier they begin to absorb this key knowledge, the less intervention will be needed later in their careers.

When pupils are expected *to recognise the place value of each digit in a three-digit number* they must do so using the terms hundred, tens and ones, a slight progression from the preceding year in the direction of being able *to recognise the place value of each digit in a four-digit number* where the term thousands is added. The concepts remain the same and, arguably, once they have moved beyond 4 digits it becomes a mere matter of continuing the pattern with the introduction of tens of thousands, hundreds of thousands and millions but for all intents and purposes 10,000,000 is the aim of the 2014 National Curriculum. If pupils have been given the appropriate diet then this becomes a reasonable expectation as the secure understanding of place value will lead to a recognition that the pattern is easily manipulated when working with tens of millions.

European influence

I was always taught that in numbers of greater value than 999 a comma should separate each of the classes but anyone brave enough to venture east of the British Isles will immediately find that there are four possible and equally mathematically accurate connotations for the division of such classes. Take the following examples for instance:

- 2 303 405,98
- 2.303.405,98
- 2,303,405.98
- 2 303 405.98

Each is mathematically accurate in the context in which is provided. Only one, as far as I am aware, is officially recognised in Britain and this includes the use of commas to separate classes and a decimal point to separate whole numbers from decimal numbers.

In somewhere such as Germany however you may be perturbed to discover that three of the four may be considered accurate, though there is no European Union think tank to provide any semblance of a definitive answer on the subject. Think of the millions that could be spent putting this particular ghost to bed!

Standards and Testing Agency and Department for Education guidance at the time of writing states that all are mathematically accurate and as such all are acceptable as test answers. The 2014 National Curriculum itself uses spaces instead of commas but some examples in the 2016 test paper samples use commas instead of spaces. At least we can be safe in the knowledge that all are acceptable to the powers that be. And rightly so!

Without a shadow of a doubt I would always recommend the use of base 10 equipment to act as a visual representation of the place value of numbers in the hope that as pupils progress and become able to manipulate the numbers increasingly fluently then the use of apparatus as a tool for creating concrete representations of abstract numbers or calculations will no longer be necessary. Even where it is necessary, and there will be some pupils who continue to need this scaffold deep into Key Stage 2, it can act as a doorway for them to access the more complex concepts in the curriculum safely and consistently.

Be sure that you embrace the visual representation as a tool that can be used to bolster pupil progress and enhance understanding because, for me, they are, and may always be, the clearest example of a bridge between the concrete and the abstract. On one bank we have one one so to speak and on the other side of the river we have the concept of the number 1. The number 1 can be represented by one one, as can the numbers 2–9, and we can show the pupils this by asking them to collect a certain number of ones. If a child holds five ones in their hand a link can be drawn with the number 5 and the numeral which has come to represent it. The discussion should always make the link explicit, five ones is the same as 5, this is an accepted truth in much the same way $1 + 1 = 2$ has been the foundation of mathematical understanding throughout the ages.

Yet there is no time to rest on this certainty as pupils must soon understand that when they have 10 ones they have one ten and that 9 is the maximum number of any unit that can be possessed by any particular unit before becoming the next unit. This may seem complex but essentially we must understand that in our base 10 system when we record numbers the value of each digit is ten times larger than that to its right and this continues into eternity. Ten ones becomes one ten, ten tens becomes one hundred, ten hundreds becomes one thousand and so on until we reach infinity and the matrix explodes. Base 10 equipment is perfect for this kind of explanation as the pupils can physically manipulate the equipment so that ten ones can be exchanged for one ten, ten tens for one hundred and so on. This will become particularly useful when pupils learn the fundamentals of calculation so it is essential that they understand the foundations of our base 10 system.

If we want to suitably challenge our pupils then, as I have said, greater numbers does not necessarily mean greater challenge and you should consider the application of place value in a different base. In the past I am told teaching would begin with base 2 and work its way up towards base 10. So why not see if your pupils are up to the challenge? Granted, binary notation has a lesser role to play in computer technology than it did at the turn of the 21st century but, as I have said before, I am assured that it still has a role to play in computer and mobile app technology. Perhaps this cross-curricular link is something you could make the most of. Certainly to any pupil I thought had mastered base 10 I would explain the fundamentals of the system, binary means the value of each place value column is twice as great as the last (in a right to left motion) and that only the digits 1 and 0 can be used due to the binary nature of the system.

I would explain that binary takes its meaning from bi which means two, hence the two possible digits and the value growing twice as great. I would record the headings in tandem with the base 10 headings. Look, 64, 32, 16, 8, 4, 2, 1, they execute the same function as M, HTh, TTh, Th, H, T, 1/Ones and this should be used in your investigation. This, I feel, provides sufficient background for any pupil working at this level to investigate what the numbers from one to twenty look like in binary form. The principles remain the same but the context grows increasingly abstract and as such your subject knowledge will play a key role in exactly how successfully you can challenge and increase the depth of learning taking place.

Symbolic importance

Eventually pupils must *compare and order numbers from 0 up to 100 using < > and = signs* and I would be wary here of your use of the crocodile[1] to signify the meaning of the symbols. The reason being that it may become problematic when the essence and meaning is attached to the crocodile rather than the sign. It may be an idea to provide a mnemonic such as pointing to the smaller number as it maintains the form of the signs without the addition of teeth or eyes. I would suggest you embrace the use of these symbols as an extension of your language, comparing and contrasting whenever possible with whoever possible. It is only in this way that meaningful connections can be made at this young age preventing any misinterpretations further in their education careers.

A popular culture reference which will no doubt allow you to date this publication: no sooner had Wayne Rooney overtaken Thierry Henry as the highest Premier League goal scorer for a single club than an opportunistic Manchester United fan had posted a picture with Rooney on one end and Henry on the other and in between was a greater than symbol. Controversial to say the least, and I must point out I follow neither club, but I did think it was an interesting way to start a maths lesson with consideration for how the symbol had been applied to this particular real life situation. A hook for boys perhaps and maybe even an explanation of extraordinary clarity but certainly I feel it represents a way of thinking about mathematical symbols in which we are not usually comfortable.

As we move through the year groups pupils must *compare and order numbers from 0 up to 1,000 before comparing and ordering numbers beyond 1,000* and while it does not specify the use of < > and = signs I still recommend their use as an effective description of comparison between numbers. It may also be useful to introduce ≤ and ≥, meaning less than and equal to and greater than and equal to, something which will raise the expectation during the comparison ever so slightly. If pupil mobility means children come to you unaware of the essence of these symbols I suggest you make it one of your priorities in the initial stages of your impact on their mathematics education.

In Year 3 it stipulates that pupils must *solve number problems and practical problems involving these ideas*. If you have entered at any other point in this book you will have noticed that I wholeheartedly recommend the use of practical application as a learning opportunity. For me it is much greater than statutory requirement, it is a measure of understanding. If pupils cannot apply then they do not truly understand and this is, as I understand it, the benchmark for the 2014 National Curriculum. Be sure that the offering is rich and varied. Ensure that word problems are taught but that they do not become the staple of the use and application taking place within your classroom. Pupils must also be allowed to apply to real life problems, potentially through educational visits or role-play and to investigate through mathematically rich tasks which can be accessed at a range of levels.

Again I would recommend you use nrich.maths.org, the NCETM website and the identification of documents which link the objectives in the National Curriculum with such investigations. The 2014 National Curriculum stipulates that pupils must *solve number problems and practical problems involving these ideas* and in Year 4 it adds that this must occur *with increasingly large numbers* and this eventually grows to become *solve number problems and practical problems that involve all of the above* (something which changes only in wording for the oldest primary pupils in Year 6). Please recognise that the increase in numbers is not a matter of differentiation, for this would not meet the aims of mathematics in general or the National Curriculum. Instead I understand it to act as a barometer of fluency which asks if pupils can work consistently correctly with such large numbers. The longer the calculation, presumably, the greater the opportunity for error and as such the greater the challenge to their consistency and efficiency. Can pupils manipulate the numbers fluently and navigate the potential pitfalls? Only true understanding and reasoning will see them through.

True differentiation can be found within the non-statutory notes and guidance. Here clear guidance is given as to what will be expected in the problems being solved, for instance, by your Year 5 pupils. While reading this particular document I would suggest you try to notice how decimal numbers and fractions will come into play even though they aren't specifically mentioned in the statutory guidance. Your problems, if accurately differentiated, will take account of this unspoken understanding. The recognition and description of linear sequences, including those with whole numbers and fractions as the example states, certainly acts as a forerunner to possible algebraic understanding and there is greater need to heed the advice of the non-statutory guidance and allow pupils the opportunity to find the term to term rules. This description of a given rule could be discovered through the use of systematic recording, a table being the most systematic method on offer at this stage, and trial and error attempts to identify patterns within the evidence recorded.

We have already discussed the *use of different representations* of numbers when considering the place value of 4-digit numbers as I believe the two are inextricably linked. Much the same as the *identification, representation and estimation of numbers* should be tied together with *rounding any number to the nearest 10, 100 or 1,000*. If you are going to estimate you will need to be able to round and so it is in this order I would introduce the concepts.

When rounding the pupils must be clear on which number is instrumental in the decision making process. This can easily be identified as the number one place to the right of the units being rounded to. For instance when rounding to the nearest 10 we must identify the value of the ones and when rounding to the nearest 10 million we must identify the value of the millions. Once they have identified the crucial digit they must know that 5 and above rounds up, 4 and below rounds down. It is very straightforward and through repetition and clear guidance pupils can easily apply this to their problem solving and *estimation* tool-kit. For if they can round they can use this to draw estimates on the total, difference, product and quotient of as many numbers as they like. This in turn allows them to check solutions to investigations and problems with a rough idea of the ball park figure they should have attained.

A somewhat cumbersome requirement asks pupils to *round any number up to 1,000,000 to the nearest 10, 100, 1,000, 10,000 and 100,000* which could probably be summed up as rounding numbers to 1,000,000 to any given power of 10. Perhaps there is a mathematical reason for this and I would happily be proven wrong in saying it could be much more succinct in its presentation of this particular objective. By Year 6 this has now been replaced by the need to *round any whole number to a required degree of accuracy*. Perhaps there was a mathematical reason for this but nevertheless we now know the expectation is there and the skills can be approached in the same way. It must be noted, however, that pupils should be able to round to any given number e.g. to the nearest 45 or the nearest 13 when rounding in Year 6, such is the expectation suggested by this requirement. What practical application it has I'm not convinced but it may play an important role in the mental calculations and method used to manipulate large numbers efficiently and mentally.

Friends, countrymen, Roman numerals

The headline grabbing formal introduction of Roman numerals as an aspect of place value as opposed to an alternative to Arabic numerals on the face of a clock comes in Year 4 and is a new addition to the requirements of the National Curriculum. Specifically pupils must *read Roman numerals to 100 (I to C) and know that over time, the numeral system changed to include the concept of zero and place value* before learning to *read Roman numerals to 1000 (M) and recognise years written in Roman numerals*. Although it may seem a tiresome burden to many, this is fantastic for those of us who love to understand the back story or the reason behind decisions of historical and mathematical value.

You see, zero came to the English language from Africa via Italy and France to represent the concept of emptiness. Zero = empty. It's that simple. The Roman number system didn't have the concept of zero and as such decimalisation would be near impossible if not downright difficult to comprehend for 8-year-old children. It also had an interchangeable system for reading numbers where sometimes, depending on the number, the position of a numeral meant subtract instead of add, for instance the number 9 is IX or one before ten. We really are much better off, in my continually humble opinion, through the use of Arabic numerals and this must be relayed to our pupils. Though, once they begin to manipulate Roman numerals I'm sure they will appreciate their good fortune.

Certainly in the run up to the introduction of the material made statutory in 2014 a highly contentious discussion and debate took place around the control politicians have over the English National Curriculum and the introduction of Roman numerals almost acted as the poster boy for this in a sense because those wary of governmental influence accused politicians of harking back to a bygone era during which they were educated, often privately, themselves. It is easy to see how this can appear the case upon an initial inspection of the curriculum but on closer analysis the key really has to lie in and around the concept of zero and the specific reference made to this understanding in the aforementioned statutory requirement. Rather than representing a backward facing approach to education it could be argued that it does in fact symbolise the fluency and confidence set out in the aims of the mathematics curriculum.

For instance, if we truly want to understand our own number system then it could be argued we can gain the most depth and insight through an analysis and understanding of other number systems and the associated processes and operations. I regularly encourage my more able mathematicians to explore base 2 in order to deepen their understanding of base 10 and perhaps the same principle is at work here with Roman numerals. Rather than focusing on that which may be useful to us in a direct way and on somewhat a daily basis, we must also consider how we can learn from the possibility that things can be done differently and what similarities exist.

I highly recommend an exploration of the Roman system of calculation and the 'calculators' used throughout the Roman Empire as an exercise in the consideration of alternative strategies. Not only does this particular area of mathematics have the potential to act as a strong cross-curricular link but it can also be used to foster higher order thinking in and around the systems we take for granted as the most efficient. If this is something you are interested in following up I recommend you deepen the offering with consideration of calculation methods in India and China, where ancient methods remain in use, with a high level of efficiency and proficiency, to this day.

If I were conducting an investigation into number systems or calculation methods I would open with the question 'Ancient Rome, China or Western Europe, which has the most effective number system?' before providing criteria which I wish the pupils to use as a guide. I may then, for instance, give calculation, ease of use, speed of use and accuracy as examples of criteria upon which a number system can be evaluated and, if the pupils are able enough, I may even ask them to create their own criteria with suitable reasoning and justification. In a moment's consideration, and with very little in the way of resources aside from a little specific subject knowledge, I've turned something which at first seemed redundant, self-serving and irrelevant into a higher order investigation which will encourage pupils to consider the strengths and weaknesses of the Arabic number system, growing ever more familiar with the key concepts as they do. You may choose to use a different leading question or scaffold it in different ways but the principles remain the same. If we think about the way we work from a different perspective or with a wider lens then we are encouraged to deepen our understanding and broaden our view of mathematics as a whole.

Pupils in Year 5, however, specifically must be able to *read Roman numerals to 1000 (M) and recognise years written in Roman numerals*. With this requirement we see one of the few remaining practical applications of Roman numerals outside of clock reading as pupils are expected to *recognise years written in Roman numerals*. Opportunities can be provided through the use of BBC programming which often features the use of such numerals at the end of its features but you may find greater value when combined with calendar work. Roman influence is infused throughout the measurement and standardisation of our seasons and as such provides the perfect context for the application of this particular skill. Naturally you will want to draw pupil attention to the months of the year with Latin prefixes and the reasons they remain yet slightly out of kilter. September, October, November and December were at one point the 7th-10th months as their names suggest but with standardisation came the introduction of two further months interspersed throughout the calendar leaving us with the current, albeit pedantic, disharmony we currently observe and the opportunity to explore, connect and apply.

It is expected that pupils know their times tables to 12×12 by the end of Year 4 and so the next logical step in the progression revolves around the manipulation of powers of 10. Not just being able to count forwards or back in the various powers but managing to manipulate, explain and control the powers, understanding the place value in large whole numbers. When explaining the concept of the power of 10 use the idea that you are multiplying by 10 once more each time and draw a link between the power and its written form e.g. 10 to the power of 3 is $10 \times 10 \times 10$, there are three tens, it is equal to 1,000 ergo 10 to the power of 3 must involve the thousands. It might be worth by this point, when you can guarantee they have had a rich diet of counting in prior years, asking pupils to arrange a counting stick lesson of their own and insisting they include the key vocabulary outlined.

What will become abundantly clear is that the requirements found in the Year 6 section of the maths curriculum are a culmination of all that has gone before them, the end product in a progression that has spanned over half the lifetime of the pupils working through it. As always the key principles remain the same and if they are applied consistently correctly misconceptions will be both prevented and addressed once identified through your increasing subject knowledge.

Whether you feel it justified or not that up to 80% of your time can be spent on one area of content, I encourage you to consider the impact of links between areas of content and to plan in advance the links you aim to make. For instance, if you want your pupils to develop their understanding of 3 digit numbers I can think of no better way to do it than by measuring liquids, for whatever purpose you desire, which automatically makes the numbers and their value meaningful. A pupil will say *I have this much liquid, quick write it down, right, what does that mean? How much more do we need?* And this will continue, inspired by your shrewd and carefully considered approach to teaching and learning about mathematics. When you consider the alternative could be a worksheet where pupils must write 3 digit numbers down, I know which one I think fosters greater mathematical fluency and understanding.

Note

1   In my experience it is commonplace for the greater and less than signs to be drawn with teeth added, causing them to take on the appearance of a crocodile which only eats the number/equation of greater value. While it may be helpful in the short term, it is a representation which actively avoids the establishment of a relational understanding of the inherent concepts and is highly detrimental to pupil progress.

5 Addition and subtraction

Once your pupils have a solid understanding of place value, even if this still requires the use of base 10 equipment as a concrete and malleable visual representation, then they are ready to develop a more formal written method in each of the four operations. Addition and subtraction have an inverse relationship and should ideally be taught first because in their role as the cornerstones of understanding they feed pupil fluency during the more complex written methods of multiplication and division. When done well all pupils, and I mean all pupils, can access these methods, invaluable to further success both in and out of the world of academia. The key, as always, is to provide adequate visual representation and use precise and accurate mathematical language as such conditions provide a veritable breeding ground for relational understanding.

The notion of equality

A prime opportunity to lay the foundations for later and greater understanding is the requirement that pupils should be taught to *read, write and interpret mathematical statements involving addition (+), subtraction (-) and equals (=) signs.* As we've discussed already it is essential that the vocabulary used accurately describes the operation, the symbol or, more specifically, the essence of the symbol. Avoid *makes* and *leaves*, embrace *is the same as, is equal to* and thrive in the mathematically accurate environment you will no doubt create. Do this well in Key Stage 1 and the benefits to be had as the children progress through the education system will be immeasurable.

Really it is unacceptable that we should use language which is convenient in our short term explanations with little to no consideration for the long term ambitions of our pupils and the education system in which they exist. The earlier we draw on our understanding of what the symbols and their descriptions mean the sooner our pupils will be able to reason fluently with them. They must know from the youngest age that equality is represented in this most humble of symbols and they must be expected to express themselves in these terms. Any deviation from this course will naturally lead to confusion when balancing equations, exploring algebraic formula and the simultaneous mental calculation of two or more processes.

Mental methods

The knowledge handed down through addition and subtraction will have a lasting effect on pupil fluency further on in the curriculum and it is, as always, key that we get it right early on. Throughout the Year 2 requirements it is made explicit that *concrete objects and pictorial representation* may, perhaps even should, be used to support mental and written calculations. Here we must be aware that the mental methods taught complement the written algorithms and vice versa. Mental methods do not develop by osmosis, certainly not effectively in any case, and must be taught discretely. One would imagine that your school would have both a mental and written policy outlining the models and methods to be taught but if that isn't the case refer to Year 1 number bonds to 20. If pupils can mentally orienteer through these then they should be able to apply them to the problems expected in Year 2. If they cannot then you know what you have to teach them. These complements will go a long way to providing the answers to many of the problems and misconceptions they have regarding *early calculation*. In actual fact the need to *derive and use related facts to 100* is present in the wording of the statutory requirements, a clear indication of their enthusiasm to promote this standard mental method in conjunction with the written calculation algorithms.

Again, in this instance it is crucial to continue to lay the foundations for a varied and mathematically rich approach to problem solving where role-play, real life application, abstract problems and the more common word problems are used to ensure pupils are able to reason with control and, most importantly, fluency. That way we can be certain they have understood the knowledge imparted and our use of consistent and accurate language has been successful. If you are unsure of how best to go about this, experiment and research but most importantly make a point of planning the opportunities with specific objectives in mind. Ask yourself how role-play might fit with the objective, how might we learn about this outside? Like questioning this will become second nature with time if you lay the groundwork early.

Insert time period here

There is likely no better role-play scenario than the shop, whether it be modern day, Tudor, Victorian, Roman, Greek or otherwise, in terms of providing a wealth of experience and allowing access to a full range of mathematical skills. In this particular instance we must be prepared to provide our pupils with opportunities to mentally calculate using the methods we choose. Cards can be used to guide pupil conversation, as can a mixed ability approach, but whatever you do be specific in the skill you ask your pupils to apply. The prices you choose, the method of payment, the recording methods allowed, will all contribute to the entire experience and the challenge on offer for the pupils taking part and the possibilities are wide and varied if time is taken to consider what you want from the role-play itself.

Largely due to the fact that any prior reference to material and objects is gone, the appendix at the end of the maths curriculum identifies the formal written methods to be taught and the removal of resources from the end of Key Stage 1 assessments, there are those baffled by the inclusion of such an expectation, myself at one point included. I can, however, see the benefit in the formalisation of the methods, particularly when they are the most efficient of their kind. Currently children will be expected to complete an arithmetic paper of calculations instead of a mental maths test and I for one welcome it because a pupil who can combine the written and mental methods will be able to complete the paper with half the difficulty of a mental maths test. That is, however, my own humble opinion and it remains to be seen how assessment will continue to develop in this most tumultuous of times.

Either way the pupils need to know the algorithms and the formalisation is ramped up in Year 3 and by the time pupils reach upper Key Stage 2 models and images may no longer be applicable. There will be an increasing complexity to the mental methods applied so it is our job to ensure they are as prepared as possible. I've seen teachers exasperated when confronted with this high expectation but I've also seen those same teachers apply the principles in this book and beam with pride when they achieve what they once thought was impossible. Never my intention to be self-satisfying or smug, it is only my aim to explain that it is possible and that the highest standards are possible with all of our children. This must be our guiding light.

Number bonds

It is essential pupils *represent and use number bonds and related subtraction facts within 20* and much like *identifying one more and one less* this finds itself as a popular overarching target and something identified for many years as a crucial lock in the mathematical learning canal. The Year 1 pupil who knows their number bonds will have much greater access to the mathematics of the curriculum and it truly is advisable that they are introduced to them in a range of ways. Perhaps a precursor to multiplication tables, pupils should be allowed to investigate and explore the number bonds and there is something to be said for having the opportunity to take part in low-stakes testing on a regular basis. While this hasn't been fashionable for many years recent research and pedagogical thinking suggests that it may be of greater benefit than first imagined. It is, however, the subject of intense debate. I'd direct you towards Twitter and similar social media sites for direct and recent evidence. In particular a post by Dr Scott Warnock (2013) entitled 'Frequent, Low-Stakes Grading: Assessment for Communication, Confidence' and Geoff Richman's 'Assessment: Lower Stakes, Raise Retention' (2015) are examples of ideal starting points when considering the impact low-stakes testing can have on learning.

The right diet

Pupils must use the formal written methods to maximise the efficiency of their calculations but this may come at the detriment of understanding if pupils have not had the correct diet, as outlined throughout the progression of calculation in this book which shares many similarities with the 2014 National Curriculum. However, I would urge you to try at all times to ensure they do understand for the sake of their mathematical careers. In the actual statutory guidance it is outlined that pupils must *perform mental calculations, including with mixed operations and large numbers* in an aid to greater fluency. What those methods are must be explicit and should be outlined in your school's calculation policy. The how in this instance is equally as important as the why.

Calculation policy

In my humble opinion, an effective calculation policy should be explicit and allow members of staff to be consistent in their approach to mathematics at all times. It should never foster misconceptions and always be based on the most relevant research and thinking of the day. If you are perturbed by anything you read in your school's calculation policy then I highly recommend you enquire as to the reasoning behind the decisions which have been made. This type of dialogue is healthy in the work place and as long as you can explain yourself clearly your colleagues should be pleased that you have expressed a valid opinion with the sole intention of improving the opportunities for all the children in your care.

If you are the person responsible for the development or upkeep of a mathematics calculation policy then you must ensure that it is a reflection of your principles and your approach to mathematics education. Of course I can point you in the right direction by highlighting mathematical misconceptions to be wary of or by identifying key areas of focus but I truly believe there is no one size fits all calculation progression and that the principles will have an enormous impact on what calculation will look like in practice. As long as the outcomes meet the high standards of the 2014 National Curriculum then I don't think anything meaningful can really be said about how the pupils got there.

With all this in mind it is important to remember that mental methods should be taught in conjunction with written methods and while the 2014 Curriculum is very clear on the written algorithms there is very little of a statutory nature with regards to mental methods. That said the non-statutory guidance does provide assistance in this respect and there are a few other places you can check for a mental progression. The most notable of which comes in the form of a document known as *Teaching Children to Calculate Mentally*, published in 2010 by the Department for Education. Within this document is a reasonable progression which you can use as a basis for any formal policy you may wish or need to create. Just because the curriculum it was based on is technically out of date does not mean that the ideas are too. You'll need to adapt the information to suit your policy and create an accurate progression but within documents such as this are the foundations for clear and concise mathematical understanding. If you remember but one thing remember, and I know I say that a lot, the conjunction of mental and written methods.

Complements to ten

For me this is a prime example of where knowledge of the complements to ten will become extremely convenient. The concept is just the same no matter which particular unit you are working with so long as the pupils are secure in their understanding of place value. If they can do this then they will easily be able to add and subtract numbers with up to four digits once they have been taught the method correctly. There remains no direct reference to bridging or exchanging but there is a link to the appendix once more which provides examples of this occurring. I recommend this be introduced in Year 3 but where this is not possible you should introduce it when you introduce the addition and subtraction of 4-digit numbers as this is likely to be the first area that will necessitate such a skill.

A formal written method

Taking addition in the first instance, it is essential that pupils understand the link between the numbers on the page and the models and images they have already established. Using the class/unit headings above the numbers and not only discussing the value but representing it visually allows connections to be made. If, for instance, you are modelling the calculation 1,356 + 2,254, place the equivalent base 10 representation below each number and physically add each column in turn. Taking the time to model cannot be overstated as it is the perfect opportunity to address possible misconceptions. A typical example would sound something like this:

> One thousand, three hundred and fifty six add two thousand, two hundred and fifty four. (Identify the written numeral and the base 10 representation, highlight the link between the two.)
>
> Always begin with the units of least value. This prevents miscalculations when bridging 10, 100, 1,000, etc.
>
> The digits further to the right of the numeral have the least value. In this case it is the ones. (You may want to make reference to the fact that when adding numbers with decimal fractions the ones will not be furthest to the right and there is a distinction to be made.)
>
> Six ones add four ones. (Physically count them out when necessary.) We have ten ones. That's the same as having one ten.
>
> Record zero as a place holder in the ones column. (Zero has no value.)
>
> Record one ten under the tens column. It will be added with the other tens. (This is a good point to model the use of an accurate and legible recording style – one digit per box is usually a good starting point which allows columns to be recorded accurately.)
>
> Once we have added the units of least value we move sequentially from right to left. In this case we add the tens next.
>
> Five tens add five tens is equal to ten tens. (Physically count them out once more when necessary.) Plus the ten accumulated when we added the ones. We have a total of 11 tens. That is equivalent to one hundred and ten.
>
> Record one ten in the tens column.
>
> Record one hundred under the hundreds column. It will be added with the other hundreds.
>
> Three hundred add two hundred, plus the extra hundred accumulated when we added the tens, is equal to six hundred. (Again physically count them out when necessary.)
>
> Record the six in the hundreds column.
>
> Finally we add the thousands.
>
> One thousand add two thousand.
>
> Three thousand. We record the thousands.
>
> The sum of the two numbers we have added is three thousand, six hundred and ten. 3,610. Three thousands, six hundreds, one ten and zero ones.

To me this is how I approach any written addition calculation, whether it involves decimals or not. It should be possible to slot into any given point in the sequence and not only address the misconceptions but predict them as well. This, like any method, becomes a matter of routine once the fundamentals have been explained and the concrete is allowed to become abstract. Without the visual representation, accurate use of language and clear sequential approach this abstraction will take infinitely longer to happen and remain much less stable than as shown. Be very aware that the expectation is that pupils are working with 6-digit numbers in a way that is fluent and efficient and that the opportunities for errors increase as the numbers do. This should be your expectation and you should make the importance to your pupils and the relevance to their lives crystal clear.

Subtraction, even though it may be more difficult or less natural to conceive than its inverse operation, can be explained and understood relationally. With suitable opportunity to have the operation modelled, and time to explore, fail and analyse, pupils will find their way to a relational understanding of written subtraction. Like addition there are pitfalls to avoid which are best described through exemplar dialogue I have used many times before:

It is possible to use the inverse to check the accuracy of calculations.
The inverse of addition is subtraction.
Record the answer to your calculation above one of the other numbers previously added. In this case three thousand, six hundred and ten sits above two thousand, two hundred and fifty four. If the answer is one thousand, three hundred and fifty six then our addition calculation is irrefutably correct. (It is still possible to use base 10 equipment to model written subtraction but be prepared to alter the equipment used based on the calculation.)
As always we begin with the digits of least value, again the ones.
Zero ones subtract four ones. It is not possible to subtract four from zero and have a positive integer as the difference.
We must exchange from the next unit in the numeral, the tens in this instance.
Place a line through the one ten, record a zero in its place then record a one to the left of the zero.
This exchange means it is possible to subtract four ones from ten ones.
The difference is six ones.
Record a six in the ones column.
As always we move sequentially from right to left.
The next class to subtract is the tens.
Zero tens subtract five tens. It is not possible to subtract five from zero and have a positive integer as the difference.
We must again exchange from the next unit in the numeral, the hundreds in this instance.
Place a line through the six hundreds, record a five in its place then record a one to the left of the zero.
This exchange means it is possible to subtract five tens from ten tens.
The difference is five tens.
Record five in the tens column.

As always we move sequentially from right to left.

The next class to subtract is the hundreds.

Five hundred subtract two hundred is relatively straightforward at this point and equal to three hundred.

Record three in the hundreds column.

As always we move sequentially from right to left.

The next class to subtract is the hundreds.

Three thousand subtract two thousand.

One thousand.

The difference between three thousand six hundred and ten and two thousand two hundred and fifty four is one thousand three hundred and fifty six.

We have been proven correct!

It is hoped that you can see the potential minefield for the encouragement of misconceptions in the language used alone. The phrases are so often interchangeable in our everyday lives and vernacular that one can be forgiven for misplacing a term or two but I can assure you that the accurate use of the vocabulary given in the example models is the most conducive to pupil progress and understanding. Stick to the script, though don't be afraid to repeat steps and hone in on exactly what your pupils need to make progress. Know your terms inside out and you will inevitably increase the speed and depth at which your pupils progress, cogitate and eventually understand.

Borrowing

Such is the positivity that emanates from this affirmative message there is a part of me that is tempted to divert your attention away from the misconception so prevalent that it almost appears to have become part of the local lexicon in the United Kingdom. Of course I must be referring to *borrowing*. There's a very good chance you'll hear someone in your school use this term and an even greater chance you were taught about it yourself. The problem is, borrowing is defined as the act of 'taking and using something with the intention of returning it' (www.oxforddictionaries.com) and you have no intention of returning anything you *borrowed* during the calculation. It's just not accurate enough and whether, like my example, you choose to replace it with the word exchange or something equally mathematically appropriate, you must insist that its use is both correct and consistent.

Where pupils do not understand, the gaps may have formed in their understanding of number some time ago. I would recommend you take the base 10 equipment, draw a visual representation and make an explicit link between the action involved in the calculation and the representation. This is what you are doing, this is what it looks like using concrete materials, and this is what it looks like using the more abstract concept of numbers. Represent the algorithm in columnar form using Dienes equipment and physically add or subtract the quantities. Model the mental processes explained in earlier sections – begin with the smallest units, the ones in this case, move from right to left, explain the value of each digit as you go and be clear about what the actual process represents.

Rounding

The same rules apply when pupils are expected to *use rounding to check answers to calculations and determine, in the context of a problem, levels of accuracy*, formal methods can be used in conjunction with rounding skills, identified earlier to be taught separately, in order to estimate using numbers rounded to the nearest given power of 10. If unsure refer to the more descriptive passage describing the use of rounding and estimation in calculation.

There must be no doubt now that you are able to see how crucial it is to continue to lay the foundations for a varied and mathematically rich approach to problem solving where role-play, real life application, abstract problems and the more common word problems are used to ensure pupils are able to reason with control and, most importantly, fluency. That way we can be certain they have understood the knowledge imparted and our use of consistent and accurate language has been successful. If you are unsure of how best to go about this, experiment and research but most importantly make a point of planning the opportunities with specific objectives in mind. Ask yourself how role-play might fit with the objective, how might we learn about this outside? In Year 5 pupils are expected to *solve addition and subtraction multi-step problems in contexts, deciding which operations and methods to use and why* and this is the same in Year 6. Everything here is encompassed in the approach outlined above and if opportunity is provided and the skills linked then pupils will make the progress necessary and meet the statutory guidance while becoming mathematicians in their own right.

When looking for deeper understanding of rounding, a wide range of opportunities are on offer and many suitable investigations exist which will help you to achieve your goal of providing sufficient depth and breadth of experience. Using a set of number cards you could play a pairs game in which the player who turns the card closest to a given number wins the trick, differentiated to include decimals where necessary, or you may offer the pupils a series of Olympic event results and ask that they be rounded in order that younger pupils may understand the results more easily.

End game

If you have delved into any of the other year groups you will no doubt see that the four operations have been merged into one section by the time they get to Year 6, largely because pupils should have covered everything already and the context of the application, fluency and efficiency of the operation is the only thing really to change here. As such the guiding principles are the same as throughout the curriculum. For this reason I have no need really to alter my advice with regards to misconceptions. The non-statutory guidance gives clear examples of the expectations; it is simply a matter of applying the guidance to the requirement. There is a saying that there are only two operations and from my own experience I believe there is some truth in this and it is worth your time considering the simultaneous use of addition and subtraction and multiplication and division.

The broken calculator

One such investigation involves the representation of a broken calculator, kaput simply because some of the buttons have fallen off. The role of the pupil will be to take given numbers and make them using only those numbers and operations available on the broken calculator. Naturally you can decide exactly what is broken and as such can differentiate between the developmental needs of your pupils. In essence pupils will have to use their knowledge and understanding in a way which is not immediately obvious to them and which requires some degree of higher order thinking and reasoning. More able pupils can and should be challenged to find alternative solutions and give explanations where possible.

Number chains

Alternatively you may wish to provide your pupils with a number chain, incomplete I might add, which will require their use of the formal written methods. This investigation can be used just as easily with multiples and factors as it can with formal calculation if the practitioner is prepared to personalise the investigation for their pupils. A number chain, in case you were wondering, is a series of numbers related to each other by the way in which the next number in the sequence is generated. Essentially it's a number sequence but with increasingly large and complex numbers in this case.

Interestingly enough though, pupils are now expected to be able to decide on an appropriate operation to help solve their problem and are even given control of the method they choose. This is no doubt a step towards total fluency and control over the operations and the pupil who can do this will be highly proficient in their use of the aforementioned methods. I recommend modelling the process, using sentence starter cues to aid the explanation process and properly train the pupils to describe their decisions as accurately as you wish them to. The more precise their descriptions the more detailed their answers and the deeper their understanding. This is crucial to the fluency and mastery required and must be treated with the utmost importance.

References

Department for Education (2010) *Teaching Children to Calculate Mentally*. Nottingham: DfE.
Richman, G. (2015) 'Assessment: Lower Stakes, Raise Retention', *Edutopia*, www.edutopia.org/blog/assessment-lower-stakes-raise-retention-geoff-richman (accessed 30 April 2016).
Warnock, S. (2013) 'Frequent, Low-Stakes Grading: Assessment for Communication, Confidence', *Faculty Focus*, www.facultyfocus.com/articles/educational-assessment/frequent-low-stakes-grading-assessment-for-communication-confidence/ (accessed 30 April 2016).

6 Multiplication and division

Initially pupils are building on the grouping and sharing of the Foundation Stage Profile and beginning to *solve problems involving multiplication and division, by calculating the answer using concrete objects, pictorial representations and arrays with the support of the teacher.* This is very similar, if not identical, to the expectations for addition and subtraction with the main difference being the lack of formal recording at this stage. The importance of these concepts for future progress cannot be stressed enough and as such we must take notice of the advisory language put forward: *doubling, quantities, arrays and number patterns.* The concept of repeated addition and subtraction must be introduced through these terms and through clear visual representation which they suggest should bolster any kinaesthetic approach to problem solving.

At this point pupils are building on the multiplication and division requirements of the Year 1 aspects of the National Curriculum and rightly so. Rather, however, than using teacher and apparatus support greater emphasis is placed on the formality of the operations in their mental and written form. It is possible this represents one of the bigger shifts in expectation in the 2014 National Curriculum and is a clear rise of aspiration. By this point pupils are expected to understand that multiplication and division are respectively repeated addition and repeated subtraction. That is to say the addition of the same number over and over again or the subtraction of the same number over and over until zero is reached. If understood as such and combined with the expectation that they *recall and use multiplication and division facts for the 2, 5 and 10 multiplication tables, including recognising odd and even numbers* they will have solid foundations on which to build.

Letters and numbers

A popular investigation related to such understanding of multiplication tables involves the calculation of times tables questions when the numbers have been replaced with letters. For example when H × A = A and H × B = B we use our understanding of multiplication to derive the fact that H must be 1 and A could be 2. H is the only constant and both calculations end with the other two letters involved. Thus if A is 2, B would logically come to represent 3. This can then be taken on into more complex calculations once an understanding of the abstract nature of the investigation is in place.

Key to mastery

Access to the rest of the curriculum will be unlimited if this skill/knowledge can be acquired and anecdotally I would go as far as to say that not mastering this particular requirement is the greatest barrier to pupil progress in any school. In the same way it is essential pupils *represent and use number bonds and related subtraction facts within 20* it is almost more important that the multiplication tables are known and understood and this represents the formalisation of that process. The Year 3 pupil who knows their times tables will have infinitely greater access to the mathematics of the rest of the curriculum and it is essential that they are introduced to them in a range of ways. If understood as such and combined with the expectation that they *recall and use multiplication and division facts for the 2, 3, 4, 5, 8 and 10 multiplication tables* (this is a summation of all previous years with 3, 4 and 8 additional to Year 3), they will have solid foundations on which to build. I strongly recommend you refer to passages pertaining to the counting stick and apply in the classroom to maintain the fluency and confidence with such multiple sequences.

The expectation that they *recall multiplication and division facts for multiplication tables up to 12 × 12* (this is a summation of all previous years with the addition of the remaining tables) means they will have solid foundations on which to build. I strongly recommend you refer to passages pertaining to the counting stick and apply them in the classroom to maintain the fluency and confidence with such multiple sequences. Pupils should be taught to *identify multiples and factors, including all factor pairs of a number, and common factors of two numbers* and if they have understood when they need to need to recall such facts then they will be both able and ready to access the maths curriculum in its entirety.

Napier's rods

Devised somewhere around the early 17th century by mathematician John Napier, Napier's bones or rods have the power to reduce multiplication and division calculations to addition and subtraction problems respectively. An investigation worthy of the brightest mind, it may be worth exploring the possible uses of the rods compared with the actual usage and the creation of an instruction manual for pupils of a given age. At the very least they are well worth playing with, exploring and using as a means to broaden mathematical experience. Pupils may believe that there is a single way to do things and that's it. Once it has been learned there is nothing else to learn. *(Though I doubt many pupils with this particular mindset actually exist in the 21st century.)* Combine Napier's rods with the Roman calculator method and other, similar, historical or cultural examples and you have the makings of a broad and balanced experience of calculation.

Primes

Similarly pupils must *know and use the vocabulary of prime numbers, prime factors and composite (non-prime) numbers*. We have already discussed the place of 1 in the world of primes and it is important pupils recognise what comprises a prime number. If they are clear in the understanding that the standard definition of a prime number usually refers to the fact that a prime number is a number which has only two factors, 1 and itself, then they will be well on their way to meeting this particular expectation. Again I would refer you to the counting stick and its many uses for assistance in developing understanding and fluency along with focused investigation and exploration. A point supported by the need to *establish whether a number up to 100 is prime and recall prime numbers up to 19*. A requirement fully supported by all prior explanation and consideration, it is also useful to consider the nature of whole numbers as factors because the introduction of decimals would leave no prime numbers at all e.g. 319 is divisible by 3.19 100 times.

Eratosthenes - was there nothing he couldn't do?

Aside from calculating the Earth's circumference to a staggering degree of accuracy, Greek mathematician Eratosthenes of Cyrene spent his spare time developing an algorithm which identified prime numbers.

A hundred square from 1-100 should act as the starting point and if pupils follow a simple process they will be sure to identify the prime numbers above and beyond the expectations of Year 6 children in England.

(For posterity we are going to strike out non-primes and circle primes.)

Initially pupils must strike out the number one because we all know that 1 is almost definitely, highly unlikely, in this instance, not a prime number. (*Please see earlier technical explanation for greater certainty.*)

2 is the first prime number so we can circle it - *but we must strike out all of the subsequent multiples.*

3 is also a prime number so it can be circled - *before its multiples are struck from the record.*

4 has already been cancelled out as a multiple of 2 so the next available number is 5 - this is prime so we can circle it - *before we strike down on its multiples with great vengeance and furious anger.*

7 is the last remaining number in the top row of the hundred square - *circle it before cancelling out its multiples.*

The numbers which remain unscathed are prime numbers! Marvellous work Eratosthenes!

Prime rib facts

The following pieces of information, or factoids if you will, pertain to prime numbers and can be used as generalisations to be investigated or as topics of mathematical discussion.

- The only even prime number is 2. All other even numbers can be divided by 2.
- If the sum of a number's digits is a multiple of 3, that number can be divided by 3.
- There are an infinite number of prime numbers.
- Every natural number greater than 1 can uniquely be written as a product of primes.

Low stakes

Pupils should be allowed to investigate and explore the tables and also have the opportunity to remember them through the use of low stakes testing. We've spoken before about how this hasn't been fashionable for many years but recent research and pedagogical thinking by those mentioned earlier does suggest that it may be of greater benefit than first imagined. It is, however, the subject of intense debate and I recommend you explore the subject in greater depth to see on which side of the line you fall. The crux of the argument may lie in the definition of the word testing I suspect but whatever your decision pupils need to know the tables, they will not be able to calculate fluently without them, and it is your responsibility to ensure they do.

The essence of equality

A prime opportunity to lay the foundations for later and greater understanding is the requirement that pupils should be taught to calculate mathematical statements for multiplication (×), division (÷) and equals (=) signs. As we've discussed already it is essential that the vocabulary used accurately describes the operation, the symbol or, more specifically, the essence of the symbol. Avoid *makes* and *leaves*, embrace *is the same as*, *is equal to* and thrive in the mathematically accurate environment you will no doubt create. Do this well in Key Stage 1 and the benefits to be had as the children progress through the education system will be immeasurable.

In addition to the language of equals we must consider the quotient and product, the origins of which have been discussed earlier and suffice to say they are deeply rooted in the essence of the words and their etymology. The product comes when we multiply, the quotient when we divide. Be sure to reinforce this and take the time to explain why in language the children will understand without diluting the mathematical value. If they begin to assimilate the language now then by the time they reach Year 4 it will have been fully absorbed into the working vocabulary. Interestingly enough the quotient refers to the number of times something fits inside something else, a rather apt description of division I might add.

Commutativity

Naturally there will come the time to explore the commutative laws of multiplication just as we did with addition, *showing that the multiplication of two numbers can be done in any order and division of one number by another cannot*. Described in much greater detail earlier we must be clear that the commutative law does not apply to division and many misconceptions can lay down roots in this particular content area. The inverse relationship between the two must be explored and pupils must know that checking your answer with the inverse should begin, in the case of multiplication, with the product of the numbers: if you divide the product by one of the factors added and the quotient is the other number then your calculation is correct. If not, a mistake has been made somewhere in one of the calculations and there is no better time than the present to explore, identify and address.

You may find that pupils struggle more with the inverse of division simply because to check a division calculation you cannot simply choose any combination of numbers, you must choose the quotient and the number of least value from the original question. For example, in the case of 280 ÷ 7 = 40, we must only use 40 × 7 in the hope that the answer is 280. Only this combination will allow you to check your answer using the inverse. This by and large causes pupils some difficulty and must be made as clear as possible. When done simply it is done best.

With pupils expected at this stage to learn to *write and calculate mathematical statements for multiplication and division using the multiplication tables that they know* we begin to see the formal introduction of written algorithms. Again they can be found alongside the addition and subtraction expectations in appendix 1 of the maths curriculum but there is much more to this particular stage in pupil development than this alludes to. As pupils must *calculate two-digit numbers times one-digit numbers, using mental and progressing to formal written methods* there is a clear statement of intent for the outcomes at the end of the year. The formal written algorithm is no doubt the most efficient but it does not necessarily lend itself to fostering the deepest understanding. Pupils who understand place value will be fine and will be able to access the end expectation but those who are not fully secure will need steps put in place.

Direct instruction

When I teach written multiplication or division I, as previously stated, take pupils from their individual starting points and draw continuous reference to previous learning to make the links between each step on the progression clear. The reason we use the grid method of multiplication is not to complicate matters or make life easier for the pupils. Quite simply it is essential that pupils understand the place value involved in the calculations and the grid method happens to be part of the most effective progression on offer at present. The grid is a vehicle for partitioning. Once it is drawn the numbers to be multiplied are partitioned and placed vertically or horizontally along the inverted axis of the grid. In Year 4 pupils are expected to *multiply two and three digit numbers by a one-digit number using formal written layout* meaning the grid method is no longer relevant to age appropriate expectations. By the time they get to Year 4, however, the expectation is that pupils no longer need to refer to the grid, such is their supposed fluency and understanding. In Year 5 they are expected to *multiply numbers up to 4 digits by a one- or two-digit number using a formal written method, including long multiplication for two-digit numbers.*

> *Example.* In this case 45 and 7 – forty and five across the top, seven down the side. As dialogue and vocabulary are key to understanding I will once again outline an example of how this should be modelled during a lesson.
>
> The numbers have been partitioned. Forty and five. Seven.
>
> (This grid has two sections, AC, BC, different to the 2-digit × 2-digit which has four sections necessitated by the partitioning of both 2-digit numbers AC, BC, AD, BD – see Figure 6.1.)

	A	B
	A	**B**
C	AC	BC
D	AD	BD

Figure 6.1

It is inconsequential where we begin but I will calculate AC first.

Forty multiplied by seven.

If I remove the place holders I am left with the calculation four x seven. This equals twenty-eight.

I record the twenty-eight. How many place holders did I remove? One. Now I replace them.

280. Forty multiplied by seven is two hundred and eighty.

Record in the appropriate grid reference.

BC is the second calculation. Five multiplied by seven. Straightforward, record thirty-five in the appropriate grid reference.

Now that I have multiplied all the possible combinations I must apply my knowledge of addition. (Use the column method, already mastered through prior teaching, to add the two answers, the total is the product of the multiplication question.) Two hundred and eighty and thirty-five.

Three hundred and fifteen.

This, however, is not the end of the progression; it is merely the one step on the long road towards formality. There is a more efficient method amidst the light at the end of the tunnel and the possibility of one more stepping stone in between where necessary. I would highly recommend moving towards the most formal written method as soon as pupils are ready to do so and often when they begin to express their dissatisfaction at the length of time it takes to complete a calculation, no matter what age, it is generally a good sign they are ready to progress. It may be the case that they are ready to move to the most formal written method shown in Figure 6.2 but where they are not it is possible to relate the grid method of the column method of written multiplication. Where the grid was used to partition initially, refer to this process with the children when modelling the more contracted method. Rather than letting them struggle in a mire of abstraction allow them to draw links between what they already know and what they are trying to learn. Each of the calculations can be given a grid reference, be warned this may overcomplicate proceedings, or you can merely point out the similarities between the two methods. Once they have recorded the answer to each calculation, allow them to record what they have done to the right of the answer.

Long multiplication

24 × 16 becomes	124 × 26 becomes	124 × 26 becomes

```
      2
    2 4
  × 1 6
  ─────────
  2 4 0
  1 4 4
  ─────────
  3 8 4
```

```
    1 2
  1 2 4
×     2 6
─────────
2 4 8 0
  7 4 4
─────────
3 2 2 4
1 1
```

```
    1 2
  1 2 4
×     2 6
─────────
    7 4 4
2 4 8 0
─────────
3 2 2 4
1 1
```

Answer: 384   Answer: 3224   Answer: 3224

Figure 6.2

As they work through the calculations make continual reference to where this would be in the grid. *What would this look like in the grid? Have you applied the correct place value to your calculation? How can you be sure of the place value? Have you used the class headings?* Constant reflection and correspondence between what is known and what we intend to know (learn) is the most effective route towards our end goal of the mastery of the most efficient method of multiplication. As they develop this method they move towards the removal of the additional notes until all that remains is the abstract understanding of the value represented at each stage in the calculation. Constant repetition is necessary and children must continually be taken from their starting points but they will get there and, through the correct use of visual representation, all children can get there. Figure 6.3[1] shows a clear progression between the grid and the next two steps in the progression towards the most efficient and formal written method.

$$
\begin{array}{rl}
32 & \\
24 & \\
\hline
8 & (4 \times 2) \\
120 & (4 \times 30) \\
40 & (20 \times 2) \\
600 & (20 \times 30) \\
\hline
768 &
\end{array}
$$

Figure 6.3

Groundwork

There may be those who are ready to head straight to the most efficient formal written method of division but I highly recommend this approach for those wishing to instil a deeper and more meaningful level of understanding than the habitual level proposed by the alternative of rote learning. Once more we will delve into an example of the modelling that must take place:

What is division?

Division is repeated subtraction.

It is the subtraction of the same number over and over and over until we reach zero. Once we reach zero we count the number of times we have subtracted and have the answer to our division calculation.

For example, 15 divided by 5 is 15 - 5 - 5 - 5 = 0. I subtracted five, one, two, three times. Fifteen divided by five is equal to three.

Now, the chunking method of division is exactly the same but on a much larger scale.

450 divided by 9.

450 divided by 9 is the same as 450 - 9 - 9 - 9 until we reach zero but we haven't got the time to do this (Have a copy of the calculation in full on a few flip chart papers to show exactly how long it would take.).

Instead we can use our knowledge of place value. 9×10 is equal to 90.

450 - 90 = 360

I must record how many times I have subtracted. 10 times in this instance.

360 - 90 = 270
I must record how many times I have subtracted. 10 times in this instance.
(Once you have subtracted 90 a further three times it is time to count the number of subtractions.)
I subtracted 9 a total of 10, 20, 30, 40, 50 times. 450 divided by 9 = 50.

Alternatively this is made more efficient through the choice to select larger chunks. In this instance I could have selected to subtract 180 because I know 9 × 20 is 180. The understanding of the pupil dictates the pace at which the calculation is solved but always encourage shorter calculations because *the fewer steps, the more accurate the answer.*

Use of misconceptions and errors

It is worth making mistakes intentionally during this process in order that pupils may work relationally with the method and work their way out of a range of scenarios. If a classroom practitioner is aware of the nuances of this, and all the other methods, then they will be in the prime position to prevent, identify and address misconceptions within and around the calculations. If the correct vocabulary is reinforced in combination with this approach then pupils will make the strides towards the more fluent and efficient bus stop method, likely called in reference to its similarity with a good old English bus stop. I feel as though I have been repeating the same key phrases continually throughout this section but, as I would in class during calculation lessons, the key aspects cannot be stressed enough. Simplicity and accurate repetition is the fastest route to fluency and efficiency which will have a lasting and meaningful effect.

Pupils, similarly, should be ready for the most efficient formal written method of division and I have already recommended and modelled an approach for those wishing to instil a deeper and more meaningful level of understanding than the habitual level proposed by rote learning. It is worth making mistakes intentionally during this process in order that pupils may work relationally with the method and work their way out of a range of scenarios. If a classroom practitioner is aware of the nuances of this, and all the other methods, then they will be in the prime position to prevent, identify and address misconceptions within and around the calculations.

The most efficient written algorithm and the progression towards it is highlighted in Figure 6.4. It should be clear that the use of mental methods combined with multiplication and division facts are an unequivocal partner to success in the written methods outlined. It is no wonder pupils are specifically expected to *recognise and use factor pairs and commutativity in mental calculations.* As we have already discussed this is of crucial importance to their understanding of the concepts inherent in the statutory requirements. Without this knowledge they will not be successful so it is clear that we must ensure our pupils have the power to apply when called upon. If commutativity has been addressed as it should have been, throughout the curriculum, then your pupils will be reasoning fluently with access to such description already. If they cannot, refer to the fact that multiplication calculations will provide the same product no matter the order of the multiples. The quotient in a division calculation does not have this luxury and the order of the numbers is key to accuracy.

Long multiplication

24 × 16 becomes	124 × 26 becomes	124 × 26 becomes

```
        2                      1 2                      1 2
      2  4                   1 2  4                   1 2  4
  ×   1  6               ×     2  6               ×     2  6
  ─────────             ───────────             ───────────
  2  4  0               2  4  8  0                 7  4  4
  1  4  4                 7  4  4               2  4  8  0
  ─────────             ───────────             ───────────
  3  8  4               3  2  2  4               3  2  2  4
                          1  1                     1  1

  Answer: 384            Answer: 3224             Answer: 3224
```

Figure 6.4

The language used must always be considered, in this case the quotient and product, the origins of which have been discussed earlier and suffice to say they are deeply rooted in the essence of the words and their etymology. The product comes when we multiply and the quotient when we divide. Be sure to reinforce this and take the time to explain why in language the children will understand without diluting the mathematical value. If they began to assimilate the language when it became developmentally appropriate then by the time they reach Year 4 it will have been fully absorbed into the working vocabulary. If not, it is your responsibility to introduce and use with the utmost accuracy.

A direct link between written and mental methods can be drawn when pupils are expected to learn to *use place value, known and derived facts to multiply and divide mentally, including: multiplying by 0 and 1; dividing by 1; multiplying three numbers*. As I have said before and will no doubt say again, the formal written methods are fully complemented by mental methods taught in conjunction. We see here the formal written algorithms in all their glory, in Year 4, meaning pupils will have had two years to hone their skills before they are to be tested on their fluency and accuracy.

Application and integer scaling

Understanding of this knowledge and these skills must then be framed within a range of contexts and opportunities where pupils can *solve problems involving multiplication and division, using materials, arrays, repeated addition, mental methods, and multiplication and division facts, including problems in contexts*. With all the discussion of increased expectation and standards it is easy to forget that we are essentially talking about 6- or 7-year-old children and how important it is to remember they must be given the opportunity to explore these concepts in a range of ways and contexts. This, I believe, is essential throughout the education system but it is clear that there is a statutory requirement for this to happen in Year 2. Plan these opportunities into your teaching sequence and ensure they are wide and varied to ensure maximum opportunity for understanding and growth. Pupils can *solve problems including missing number problems, involving multiplication and division, including positive integer scaling problems and correspondence problems in which n objects are connected to m objects*. In real terms I would recommend the programme 'Mathematical Allsorts' as a means to develop reasoning and understanding of this particular statutory requirement.[2] The resource is differentiated and comes with sufficient variety to engage pupils multiple times. I am sure there are other such programmes available, this just happens to be my preference and one I know you can count on in the field.

When pupils are similarly expected to *solve problems including using the distributive law to multiply two-digit numbers by one digit, integer scaling problems and harder correspondence problems such as n objects are connected to m objects*, only a slight adjustment has been made to the expectation but it's an adjustment all the same. A somewhat more precise variant of the aforementioned requirement perhaps but I merely mention it to reinforce the notion that the statutory guidance is always useful for those unsure and should regularly be used as a point of clarification and reference.

You should not be put off by seemingly complex *integer scaling* buried deep within this particular objective. It merely refers to the kind of problems you are surely familiar with in which a given integer is scaled upwards depending on a given frequency. This often manifests itself in problems such as: John has 1 cake, it cost him 20p, how much will 5 cakes cost? Role-play and word problems will both meet the needs of the pupils who are ready to apply and the context can be made increasingly abstract through the introduction of variables such as scale. I would suggest it may be worth doubling up any fundraising activities taking place, which in my experience often include the sale of buns etc., by allowing pupils to develop a pricing strategy in the aim of achieving a particular target with a set amount of stock.

Pupils should have already explored the commutative laws of multiplication in Year 2 and Year 3 when pupils were *showing that the multiplication of two numbers can be done in any order and division of one number by another cannot*. Reference is now made to this in the statutory guidance when explaining the mental methods to be used to complement the written algorithms and, as described in much greater detail earlier, we must be clear that the commutative law does not apply to division and many misconceptions can lay down roots in this particular content area. The inverse relationship between the two must be explored and pupils must know that checking your answer with the inverse should begin, in the case of multiplication, with the product of the numbers: if you divide the product by one of the factors added and the quotient is the other number then your calculation is correct. If not a mistake has been made somewhere in one of the calculations and there is no better time than the present to explore, identify and address.

The broken calculator

As we mentioned earlier the use of a broken calculator can be quite effective when extending pupil understanding of calculation and this applies to multiplication and division as much as it does to addition and subtraction. Naturally you can decide exactly what is broken and as such can differentiate between the developmental needs of your pupils but the range of solutions you ask pupils to provide will no doubt enhance the quality of response and extend the most able of pupils.

Alternatively you may decide that you want them to create a similar problem which will not only assess their understanding of the mathematics but of the problem solving processes as well.

Number chains

Alternatively you may wish to provide your pupils with a number chain, incomplete I might add, which will require their use of the formal written methods. This investigation can be used just as easily with multiples and factors as it can with formal calculation if the practitioner is prepared to personalise the investigation for their pupils. Be careful not to mistake application of one for the other, however. Ensure that the mathematics you believe necessary to complete the number chain is indeed that which you intend it to be. Whether you want multiples and factors to be assessed or the use of formal written algorithms be sure to check that the focus area is the primary strategy for solving the problems on offer.

You will note that, just above, I have provided an example of the most efficient written method with the warning that unless the fundamentals presented in the methods outlined are in place the pupil will have no chance of establishing the relational understanding we desire for them. Perhaps habitual understanding is a possibility but this, for me, is as useful to a true mathematician as the proverbial chocolate tea pot. Keep it clear, accurate and take them from their starting points. Whichever approach you decide to take it is key that you maintain a consistent use of vocabulary and take both the quantity value and column value into account when executing calculation algorithms.

Notes

1 With thanks to the University of Cumbria: http://ictedusrv.cumbria.ac.uk/maths/SecMaths/U1/page_20.htm.
2 Mathematical Allsorts is available to buy at www.atm.org.uk/shop/Mathematical-Allsorts/act072. For non-members the price is currently £22.00 but for members the cost is reduced to £16.50. A range of differentiated problem solving opportunities are provided which require little to no knowledge of number and focus on the thinking skills necessary to negotiate mathematical problems.

7 Fractions

Throughout my teaching career, particularly during any professional development which had a focus on mathematics, the importance of a relational understanding of fractions has been continually stressed. If there is one aspect of mathematical understanding which I've been led to believe is crucial to pupil growth it is that study of values which form the part of one whole and the various representations and connotations we find in the world around us. So it was no surprise to me, and I'm sure to many others, that Fractions, with a capital F it must be noted, came to form a key part of the 2014 National Curriculum in England. So much so that a clear progression can be drawn throughout the document and those of you working with this particular document will notice it was given its own 'section' on which we must focus our efforts. The importance and coverage is noticeably greater than in previous versions of the curriculum and the mathematics should therefore be given consideration to ensure we deliver, not only as intended, but to the greatest end for our pupils.

And while I am all for the increased weighting which fractions have come to enjoy, a slight caveat must be added to this in as much as it is worth contemplating what we lose in cross-curricular/inter-disciplinary convergence. As teachers we must be aware of the relationship between fractions and division, of the humble beginnings we find in the early years, where sharing forms the very foundations upon which we will build throughout their educational careers. When teaching fractions or providing opportunities for pupils to learn, discover and explore, be sure to know where the links in the curriculum are and to treat the relationships with the respect they deserve. If you do then you will make your job much easier than someone treating them in isolation. Yes there are skills to be explicitly taught and there are links between areas which may not present as immediately obvious but they are essential to pupil development and finding the true depth of progress and understanding we desire.

Counting up and down in tenths

For instance if I were a Year 3 teacher and I were to teach *counting up and down in tenths*, as is the required standard for that year group, if I had not already provided pupils with a sound understanding of *place value of three digit numbers* then I would be unable to use the model and images necessary to highlight the link between the concrete and the abstract. It would be my intention to use the base 10 equipment which, if we were working in whole numbers, represents 1,000. It is a cube and is comprised of 1,000 ones. When teaching the relativity of decimal place value I would use this 'thousand' as 1 whole. Therefore, what was previously used to represent 100 would become one tenth because it takes ten of them to make 1 whole, ten becomes a hundredth because it takes one hundred of them and the ones become thousandths because, you guessed it, it takes one thousand of them to make one whole. Without prior, and often simultaneous, understanding of the model, image and overall place value then I cannot expect the pupils to take this new leap towards an understanding of place value where the fractions are less than one whole.

I feel the entire curriculum must be considered in this way: where does the necessary prior knowledge lie, where are the links between fundamental principles and inextricably linked concepts and what can I do to ensure that I am providing the conditions most conducive to pupil progress because with the increased weighting must come an increased sense of importance to the development of our pupils.

Equal parts

Initially, at the beginning of Key Stage 1 usually, pupils should be taught to *recognise, find and name half as one of two equal parts of an object, shape or quantity* and to *recognise, find and name a quarter as one of four equal parts of an object, shape or quantity*. The fundamental principle at stake is the nature of fractions as *equal* parts of a whole. Pupils must be given the opportunity to realise that the equivalence of the size of each quarter or half is the very crux of the concept and that unequal fractions cannot even be considered quarters or halves at all. I'm sure we've all seen, or certainly will see, examples of pupils colouring grossly unequal 'halves' of a rectilinear shape and considering job done, target achieved, let's tidy up and get on with play time, only for us to realise that in fact a fundamental misconception is afoot. However you present the concept, which can even sometimes involve the delicious pizza, the equivalence must form the root of both your dialogue and questioning. I often find it best to have the pupils make whatever it is you want them to share evenly during the next session. In these sessions it is often difficult to get exactly half so you must insist that it acts only as a construct upon which to build the understanding necessary so that when you move from the concrete to the pictorial the pupils come along with you and take the concept of equal fractions on board. As long as they wash their hands first!

This is relatively straightforward and I would not blame you for wondering exactly how this skill can be developed and opportunity for greater depth provided. Those of you in this frame of mind should find the following investigation an excellent resource for challenging your most able pupils and finding the depth expected by the revised standards of the National Curriculum.

Shaded shapes

The problem itself requires pupils to find ways to shade half of a shape in any other way than the bog standard horizontal, diagonal and vertical splits we see so frequently. You may choose to use an interactive white board slide or PowerPoint presentation to support your explanation of the problem and help your pupils to visualise what is expected. The key, however, is that you can introduce the idea of lateral thinking to the point at which you feel your pupils will be ready to access the problem. There is no need to show them all the possible solutions, but rather give them a fleeting glimpse of an idea and allow them to crack on with the investigation while you observe both their interactions and their ideas. A clearer example of extending and deepening the challenge rather than accelerating pupils towards $\frac{1}{3}$, $\frac{1}{5}$, $\frac{1}{6}$ and so on does not exist in my humble opinion.

In England, pupils in Year 2 pupils should be taught to *recognise, find and write fractions* $\frac{1}{3}$, $\frac{1}{4}$, $\frac{2}{4}$ *and* $\frac{3}{4}$ *of a length, shape, set of objects or quantity*. Building on the understanding of equivalency within halves and quarters, pupils need to see the link between the written form of a fraction and the physical incarnation. Again it should be explicitly clear that the fractions must be equal parts of the one whole, e.g. thirds are three equal parts of one whole, and this should be your main aim when questioning pupils about their understanding. Pupils must be given the opportunity to realise that the equivalence of the size of each third, quarter or half is the very crux of the concept and that unequal fractions cannot even be considered thirds, quarters or halves at all. There are a plethora of visual representations in a multitude of dimensions, fraction walls, towers, circles, dominoes, stamps, puzzles and even frog ponds, whatever they are, included, which can aid the development of the concept of fractions and you can't really go wrong with any of them as long as you get the fundamental principles right. Equivalence relieves ambivalence.

You might choose to use a similar problem to the one mentioned above involving shading shapes with the added twist that the pupils are trying to shade a range of fractions, $\frac{1}{3}$ or $\frac{1}{5}$ for example, or you may wish to venture slightly off topic and provide a deeper understanding of fractions without making direct reference to the specific understanding outlined in this particular objective.

Cube investigations

One of many investigations featuring their use, such a venture may require pupils to explore a shaft of interlocking cubes and consider how many cubes they need to make a rod three or four times longer and a half and a quarter the length. They may then wish to take photographs of their solutions and have other pupils match the solution to the photograph. All the while challenging their peers, and themselves, at a greater depth than first anticipated.

When developing ideas for possible extensions and support, key questions for developing understanding must also be considered so they can be provided for the pupils and used to enhance the dialogue which takes place during the problem solving process.

With this in mind, the only question really is one of suitability for your pupils. I would imagine both of the aforementioned problems to be pitched at a level which would certainly cover the expected understanding of a Key Stage 1 pupil. That is not to say that some Year 3 pupils will not benefit from, or some Reception children would not be able to access, them, but rather it is a reminder that your knowledge of the pupils in your class is essential in determining how you present the investigations and the scaffolding you will need. An admonition which must be attached to all of the problems and investigations covered in this book.

Throughout this process, we must begin to make explicit the link between the written and physical forms the fractions take. During any guided input I insist that you refer to the model or image chosen and the written form. Make it clear, though not legally necessary, what the numerator and denominator are so that pupils begin to assimilate the necessary vocabulary to succeed as they continue through the progression. Highlight the fact that you have divided the shape or quantity into four equal parts, this is the denominator, *look I have written four to represent it*. Equally, highlight the fact that you have shaded, coloured, eaten, whatever it may be two of those parts, this is the numerator, the number of those parts we are using, *look I have written two to represent it*.

If we successfully highlight the link between the written and physical forms of fractions we will have begun to prepare the pupils for *writing simple fractions for example $\frac{1}{2}$ of 6 = 3 and recognising the equivalence of $\frac{2}{4}$ and $\frac{1}{2}$*. It is necessary to make the link explicit and as important to give pupils the opportunity to explore both the recording and concept of fractions. Equivalency between recorded fractions can only come when the concept of the separate fractions in reality, in concrete, are clear and embedded. Opportunity to apply their knowledge and explore through investigation will allow the similarities to be drawn out through skilful questioning. A pupil who knows the 2 times table, as mentioned in a prior statutory requirement, will have a greater advantage in trying to see the link between $\frac{1}{2}$ and $\frac{2}{4}$ than a pupil who does not. Though the same may be said for those who can double and halve, the mental agility necessary to see such a connection sits easier with me when linked to knowledge of the times tables at this particular age. If you effectively ensure that pupils can manipulate fractions in a variety of ways and draw explicit links between written and physical forms then you will have provided sufficient opportunity for the concept to embed securely.

Pairs

I can easily imagine a pair based card game as something which can be manipulated and developed to provide suitable challenge at this stage in your pupils' development. The game in question often requires pupils to match pairs of cards with the same value. The cards sit face down and each player must only turn over two at a time, keeping any pairs they may find. A game with which most people will be familiar, no doubt, but there are many versions which can be made to suit the needs of the pupils.

When matching such a game with the requirements and objectives we are currently discussing I would imagine that the form taken by each card will be somewhat dissimilar to its pair. For example pupils may match quantities of money, e.g. half of £2 with a £1 coin, or the written form of fractions with the pictorial representation of a number.

This, in my opinion, can very easily be made into a physical card game where the pairings are chosen by you to match the developmental level of your pupils. There is no reason why half to £2 can't become ½ of £2 and thus matching the activity securely to the requirement of the National Curriculum expectation. It merely depends on how you want to challenge your pupils and the level at which they can access the mathematics.

In England, a preface given to all of the requirements directly referenced, Year 3 pupils should be taught to *count up and down in tenths; recognise that tenths arise from dividing an object into 10 equal parts and in dividing one-digit numbers or quantities by 10*, whereas in Year 4 pupils should be taught to *count up and down in hundredths; recognise that hundredths arise when dividing an object by one hundred and dividing tenths by ten*. A clear progression can be drawn and immediately it cries out that the ever versatile counting stick can and must be utilised. Much like the use of whole numbers counting in tenths can, and possibly should, be taught without any formal lesson structure and introduced through daily counting using the aforementioned counting stick. Use of the language of decimal fractions as well as fractions will open up greater dialogue and understanding, drawing connections with future and previous learning.

Visual representations

When counting, instead of using multiples, powers of ten or sequences relevant to the developmental expectation, the class teacher can provide opportunity for pupils to experience the visual representation of sequences of fractions. The link between the visual representation and the numbers, it is widely felt, will allow pupils to utilise both the left and right sides of the brain and as such forge considerably stronger links than without. The general consensus is that while the right side of the brain takes care of the visual representation, the left hand side can focus on the numerical side of things and the written representation. I do not claim to be a neurological expert by any stretch of the imagination but I have seen first-hand the impact use of the counting stick can have across the entire primary phase and as such feel compelled to share my experience in the hope that it will support your pupils' understanding too.

When using the counting stick in this way it may be an idea for pupils to label the division themselves, in groups, independently, perhaps even drawing or making their own counting sticks. This could allow direct equivalencies to be drawn between fractions, decimals and percentages and their representations, building one layer of understanding on another until the pupils are secure in their knowledge of this most essential of mathematical concepts. Begin with fractions and establishing the sequences but do not be afraid to build as they progress and use counting as a precursor to guided input further down the line, even if that may be some years ahead. If you do this then you will have taken into account what I believe to be many of the key factors we must take note of when trying to enhance the connections made in the brain. For me this represents the essence of learning.

Discrete set of objects

If you looked at the Year 3 curriculum and saw pupils are expected to *recognise, find and write fractions of a discrete set of objects* using *unit fraction and non-unit fractions with small denominators* I wouldn't blame you for scratching your head and wondering exactly what this meant. In its most digestible form this simply means fractions where 1 is the numerator e.g. $\frac{1}{2}$ (a unit fraction) or a fraction where 1 is not the numerator e.g. $\frac{3}{4}$ (a non-unit fraction). There is a distinction to be made between the two types of fraction and it highlights the importance of the use of language. Through the use of these descriptions I can make a much more precise explanation or instruction than if the only term were fraction. Pupil understanding is thus enhanced and their ability to reason subsequently extended. When you are giving any sort of input or taking part in any conversation regarding fractions be sure to use these terms fluidly and explain them to pupils in order that they too may describe their understanding with the expected fluency and confidence.

Food and fractions

A useful investigation to access at this point, though not exclusively as it could be accessed at a variety of points, may be a problem which involves the sharing of food through the application of mathematical knowledge, skills and understanding. This delicious investigation could involve: a picnic, a Tudor banquet, a Viking/Celtic feast, or any other meal of your choosing, the food at which your pupils must share equally among a given number of people. Keep it specific and be clear about the number of people in attendance at the meal. Can your pupils tell us what each of them will have and can they explain how they solved the problem?

If I were planning on using this investigation to deepen my pupils' understanding of *unit fraction and non-unit fractions with small denominators* I would make constant reference to these terms throughout the process. This way pupils would have no excuse but to assimilate the necessary language and reinforce key concepts while exploring a deeper understanding of fractions and their real life application.

Use of diagrams

Eventually your pupils will need to be fluent in *recognising and showing, using diagrams, equivalent fractions with small denominators*, which will no doubt utilise the foundations laid in previous years regarding the use of the term equivalence and the role of the equals sign will keep your pupils in good stead for what is to come. Understanding what is meant by equivalent is immeasurably valuable in this situation and will allow your pupils to explore the fractions as they stand. You must ensure their prior knowledge also includes the concept of fractions as parts of a whole as outlined in previous year groups. If they can then they will have no trouble making the link between the numbers which are equivalent and the fractions which are equivalent. The use of diagrams will no doubt aid understanding and is worded specifically in the requirement yet this can be done through drawing the link between fractions of real life objects and pictures of those objects, moving towards fractions of shapes and how they are recorded. In each instance I would discuss the object, *look at this cake it is in quarters, this cake is in halves, we can see two quarters are equal to one half*, and allow pupils to explore. Then I would say, *look at this picture of the cakes, see how the diagram represents what you have in front of you* and as pupils began to make the link I would draw attention to the link between the object, the diagram and the written fraction, *see how these fractions describe the diagrams, notice they are equivalent and the relationship between the numbers.*

The very picture of equivalence

For me any investigation on equivalence would not be complete without the use of the fraction wall, which I might add, is the perfect embodiment of exploration via the use of diagrams, models or images.

To use the fraction wall successfully you must develop questions suitable for challenging understanding and the explorations of potential 'rules', something which won't hurt the development of their reasoning skills if modelled and structured correctly. You could, for instance, ask pupils to find equivalencies in a group of fractions and to represent them using the fraction wall as a basis for any reasoning.

By this stage reasoning should start to take on a more sophisticated form, though not to the extent one would expect at the far reaches of upper Key Stage 2 quite yet, and pupils should be using increasingly complex mathematical vocabulary. Though you are no doubt aware this is something I insist upon at any stage.

In addition, it should be noted here that you will also want your pupils to eventually understand the fractional, decimal and percentage representations and as such you should pepper the investigation with plenty of opportunity to rehearse and develop the required understanding. Otherwise they'll be 13 years old and still wondering why 12.5 is $1/8$ and why a $1/3$ appears to never end in decimal form.

The same principles of delivery and provision of opportunity apply when *adding and subtracting fractions with the same denominator within one whole* and *comparing and ordering unit fractions, and fractions with the same denominators* becomes your primary concern. You will naturally want to make sure the pupils are aware of the terms numerator and denominator, the denominator being the total number of parts created from the whole and the numerator, the number of parts being considered in a particular instance. Pupils need to see the patterns, they need to physically manipulate the fractions and they need to explore and question at their own pace. The more relevant you can make this, through the use of money perhaps, the more meaningful and concrete it will become. Hopefully you should be able to build on the foundations laid in previous years but where you don't, refer to the progression and address gaps in learning. The language built up over the years preceding your own year group are key, this has been stressed throughout. If the gaps exist, go back and fill them.

Families of equivalent fractions

As the expectation increases so too does the nature of understanding and the depth at which pupils are expected to operate. Whereas in the past pupils would have been expected to identify equivalencies the 2014 expectations relate to the recognition and identification, using diagrams, of *families of common equivalent fractions*. To be able to do this one must have a relational understanding, not only of the fractions and their equivalencies but also the relationship between the different families. It is no longer acceptable to know which are equivalent, the pupil must also be able to manipulate and mould as they so choose in order to show true fluency.

Taking it further

You may wish to consider using a problem similar to those mentioned before but changed ever so slightly to extend and deepen the understanding of pupils working with a few of the most recently mentioned statutory requirements and concepts. Where our work with the fraction wall focused on straightforward equivalencies, pupil understanding can be extended that bit further by asking pupils to compare fractions with different denominators and explaining how they worked it out. This may be a skill that pupils will grow to need as they make their way through Key Stage 2 but it cannot be stressed enough how this provides opportunity for those who are ready throughout the Key Stage to access challenging and enriching mathematical material.

The need for deeper pupil understanding is brought into play again, as if it were ever out of play, in Year 4 when pupils are expected to *solve problems involving increasingly harder fractions to calculate quantities, and fractions to divide quantities, including non-unit fractions where the answer is a whole number.* An objective clearly outlined in the accompanying notes and guidance, pupils must be aware of the connections between non-unit fractions, multiplication and division of quantities and focus on tenths and hundredths in particular. For me the real key here is that all areas of prior understanding and knowledge are brought together, the relationship between all the various aspects of fractions and decimals covered so far is highlighted and made relevant in each other's contexts. A sound understanding of this and the multiplication and division facts mentioned earlier is the keys to success when problem solving with fractions. As always, ensure your problems are rich and varied, some closed, some open ended and continually challenging for all.

Marble malfunction

Available at nrich.maths.org, 'Andy's Marbles' may provide the perfect opportunity for the added richness and depth I'm continually harking on about and, certainly with the right tweaks, could be made accessible for a broad range of pupils across Key Stage 2. An example of the relationship between fractions and multiplication, 'Andy's Marbles' involves an unfortunate bag malfunction and the need to organise the madness which usually ensues after such an event. Your pupils must help Andy and are provided with an opportunity to apply their knowledge and all-important reasoning skills while doing so. The usual support is provided for teachers, with scaffold, extensions, possible approaches and background on the problem all provided along with documents which will aid the recording and thinking processes.

Decimal equivalents

One would have thought that the identification of equivalent fraction families would have covered the recognition of *decimal equivalents of any number of tenths or hundredths or decimal equivalents to* ¼, ½, ¾ and perhaps the only difference is the expectation to write them as well. We are, however, advised that the simplification of fractions is appropriate at this stage in the progression and this is a clear differentiation from the aforementioned requirements. Again, understanding what is meant by equivalent is immeasurably valuable in this situation and will allow your pupils to explore the fractions as they stand. You must ensure their prior knowledge also includes the concept of fractions as parts of a whole as outlined in previous year groups. If they can then they will have no trouble making the link between the numbers which are equivalent and the fractions which are equivalent. Eventually, hopefully before the end of the year, your pupils will be able to draw these simplifications without reference to a model, image or visual representation.

The maths of chocolate

The mother of all fractions investigations, and certainly my personal favourite, is one known throughout the land involving the use of some strategically placed chocolate bars. Linked to both Key Stage 2 and Key Stage 3, possibly because of the potential to describe any outcomes using complex algebraic formulae, this a problem which could quite possibly be used as an assessment opportunity with pupils aged around 10 or 11 years of age, though I've seen it perplex teachers, myself included, when the full mathematical power is unleashed.

Children are presented with three tables, each with one more chocolate bar than the one before, to a maximum of 3, and asked to consider which table it is best to sit at if the chocolate is to be shared equally between the people sitting at each table at that moment in time.

(*I thought long and hard about that particular description but really that was my less than hoi polloi way of saying there are three tables; one has one bar of chocolate, one has two bars of chocolate and one has three bars of chocolate.*)

The problem posed to each child changes depending on the order in which they, one at a time, enter the room and make their decision, as each is intent on securing the greatest prize possible.

For example: the first child chooses the table with three chocolate bars because there they will get to eat all three bars. The second child should choose the table with two chocolate bars as there they will get two bars to eat. The third child, however, also chooses the three bar table because there they will get one and half bars of chocolate compared with the bar on offer at each of the other tables.

While this takes place mathematical reasoning, understanding of fractions, decimals even, and problem solving strategies should be drawn out through lengthy, detailed and engaging discussion. I add the last adjective simply because there may be negative connotations surrounding the use of the term lengthy but I firmly believe that if children are engaged then the discussion is paramount to their development.

Who knows, they may eventually be able to describe it algebraically.

Of course you should use your professional judgement as you will know your children best but let it be known that you must draw out as much as possible in preparation for the post investigation analysis which will come in three distinct parts. Pupils must compare different methods and say which they thought were best and why before considering the possibility of approaching a similar challenge with the knowledge they have acquired during this investigation.

The depths from which this one simple problem can draw is, in my opinion, immense and almost unfathomable but I must stop before I digress into entirely hyperbolic rhetoric. Suffice to say the knowledge of fractions pupils will exert when solving this problem is exactly what's needed to give your pupils' grey matter a proper workout. And, if you feel your subject knowledge limits stretched, this is a popular investigation regularly discussed online where there are many possible solutions to consider.

Long before pupils come to understand decimal place value they will have been introduced to the concept of multiplying and dividing by 10. Somewhere around the time they learn to use a less formal method of multiplication they will have to understand the power and role of 0 as a place holder. In the past people often said add a 0 or add two 0s when multiplying by 10 and 100. This is completely and utterly mathematically inaccurate and they should always be encouraged to move the digits right or left depending on whether you are multiplying or dividing and to use zero as a place holder where necessary. Thus it is with this in mind that I find it surprising that the first mention of *finding the effect of dividing a one or two digit number by 10 and 100, identifying the value of the digits in the answer as ones, tenths and hundredths* comes in Year 4 and in the relation to fractions.

For me it is a key aspect of understanding place value and I would recommend it be involved earlier even if it is not statutory. In some respect I can see why it has been included as the authors want pupils to see the relationship between fractions and decimal fractions and to be able to manipulate numbers and work within ones, tenths and hundredths. The principles above are the same for multiplying any number, integer or fraction, and should be applied in the same manner. To do so is to ensure pupils continue to develop their understanding of the concepts we wish them to master. It may be of worth to consider that the decimal point is a static entity in these calculations and pupils who understand the role of 'der punkt' are those who will be able to reason fluently more easily and manipulate decimals in calculations much more readily than those who do not.

Thousands of opportunities

With regards to opportunities to deepen pupil understanding of multiplying by 10 I recommend you look no further than the investigations which I explored in greater detail when we took the time to consider number and place value. At this point in their progression, however, I believe a tweaked version of a common classroom game could help to enhance pupil understanding and fluency when exploring the effect of multiplication and division on decimal place value.

Given cards with the digits 0-9 and a range of problems designed to meet your mathematical needs, it is merely a case of tailoring your version of the game to your desired outcomes. You may, for example, wish your pupils to create the largest decimal number, the decimal closest to a given number or decimal or even to multiply numbers created by 10, 100 or 1,000. This very straightforward idea provides a wealth of opportunity for investigation and the necessary deepening of understanding.

We have already considered the language and symbols of comparison so when we think of *comparing numbers with the same number of decimal places up to two decimal places* we must continue to reflect on the mnemonics we use to help pupils remember the concepts, ensuring they are clear and mathematically accurate. We must also deliver the concept of decimal place value as a continuation, if this has not already happened, of the place value laid down throughout the National Curriculum.

I have spoken about the use of base 10 equipment, with the use altered slightly, and how it can apply just as well to decimal place value as it does to whole numbers. In my example, you may recall, what was previously used to represent 100 would become one tenth because it takes ten of them to make one whole, a ten becomes a hundredth because it takes one hundred of them and the ones become thousandths because it takes one thousand of them to make one whole. This, however, is not the only representation you can use. It is possible to use, or even make, poker chip like tokens emblazoned with various units of place value and used to represent numerical values in much the same way base 10 equipment is used. Effective use of the resources, and there are many more not mentioned in this brief paragraph, will consist of continual reference between the abstract and the concrete and direct links being made between what the pupils already know and what they need to know next.

Prudency is essential here because even though the resources can be used to develop understanding, it can only happen if pupils are clear in their understanding of whole number place value first. This must be fully secure and pupils should have released themselves from the scaffold provided by base 10 equipment or equivalent resources. If you use the visual representation and the previous concepts are not clearly defined then they will not work a second time, things will become muddled and learning skewed. Be sure to assess pupil understanding before you undertake any such action in the classroom and be sure to refer to previous place value explanations to ensure accuracy of language and mathematical procedure.

Solving simple problems

The problems outlined when pupils are expected to *solve simple measure and money problems involving fractions and decimals to two decimal places* have inadvertently been covered in previous discussions/explanations on problem solving and the application of skills and knowledge. The only difference really is the complexity of the level at which pupils must access the decimals. In reality decimals to two decimal places are a reflection of everyday financial transactions. If pupils have been given the proper diet and allowed to explore money as recommended then I suspect it will just be a matter of relating the contextualised to the abstract for they should have been completing similar transactions throughout their education careers. What's to be done if they have not? Fill the gaps. Identify the weaknesses and plug the holes with high quality teaching and learning experiences.

At first glance this is likely to manifest itself in the form of word problems, largely because, in my experience, teachers are usually extremely comfortable with this measure of pupil use and application of mathematics and this alone. A sweeping generalisation perhaps, but I have seen nothing in my experience to contradict this assertion. I would love to stand corrected and to be shown that sufficient depth and breadth of problem solving opportunities are consistently available for pupils in the majority of classrooms but that day has not yet come. Certainly there is a place for word problems, particularly as the standardised tests currently provide ample opportunity and need, but we must consider the necessity to broaden pupil horizons and really analyse the problems we provide and decide whether or not they meet the needs of our pupils.

Ever increasing decimal places

Easier said than done with the workload I am all too aware teachers can regularly expect to carry but this, I feel, is a classic case of working smarter rather than harder. When we look at *solving simple measure and money problems involving fractions and decimals to two decimal places* I see the opportunity for role-play first and foremost. What is your overarching topic, can financial transactions be linked to it, and if not, does your role-play area lend itself to such trading situations? If you don't have a role-play area I suggest you spend some time looking into the effective creation and use of such areas, if not for mathematical purposes (to which great ends can be achieved), then for the oracy skills it is so essential to develop.

Role-play

If we consider a few possible topics and role-play areas which link in nicely with our objective we could begin with the Romans, Greeks, Egyptians, Tudors, any ancient or historical civilisation really, and the creation of a market stall set in this time. Fill it with produce you would expect to find there and develop situations, planned carefully by the teacher, which will require pupils to apply the relevant skill. If you are learning about the Victorians you may want to have a train station, toy shop, Bob Cratchit's workbench complete with coal-less fire or even a horse and carriage depot of sorts, anything, in fact, the imagination can conjure which will eventually provide opportunity for financial transaction or the application of mathematical skills in a real-world context.

The same principles and methods should then be applied whatever the cross-curricular, overarching, umbrella topic you choose. As we've said already, markets have always been popular throughout the ages but equally so humans have enjoyed creating and with creation comes a level of accuracy that can only be achieved through the application of mathematics. In real terms it is simply a matter of taking what you know about a subject, context or time period and considering how mathematical skills can be developed through a series of imagined scenarios.

The examples I have given should start you off, of this I have no doubt, but a simple internet search will provide resources, discussion on the use of role-play and ideas if you take the time to look. You may even decide to ask your colleagues because, when it comes to generating ideas, the more brains you have, the more ideas you're going to generate. Not knowing your colleagues, I cannot attest to the quality of the ideas you may eventually generate but a start is a start and, after all, experience is the name we give to our mistakes. So go out and experiment, generate wildly creative ideas and hone the best, and most productive, until you have a back catalogue of role-play ideas to last you a lifetime.

Mental application

Pupils may have to connect equivalent fractions less than one that simplify to integers with division and other fractions less than one to division with remainders, using the number line and other models, and move from these to improper and mixed fractions. Yet if they are fully aware of the concept of the fractions they work with they can easily apply their mental multiplication and division skills to halve the time needed to solve just such a conundrum. If they are shown using practical materials and examples, the concept of mixed fractions, then they will have considerably less trouble understanding than if they are left as an abstract concept with no grounding in the real world.

Equally we can see that when pupils must connect multiplication by a fraction to using fractions as operators (fractions of), and to division, building on work from previous years, this relates to scaling by simple fractions, including fractions less than one and where the scaling principles from Year 4 apply quite naturally. Though as always, as long as pupils understand the concept of the fraction and how exactly the mixed fractions have come about, drawing on the practical first-hand experiences and models and images of earlier chapters, then they will begin to build solid foundations in these aspects as well.

The addition and subtraction of fractions

Look at the non-statutory guidance and you will see that pupils should practise adding and subtracting fractions to become fluent through a variety of increasingly complex problems. They must extend their understanding of adding and subtracting fractions to calculations that exceed one as a mixed number and continue to practise counting forwards and backwards in simple fractions. This is all covered in the requirements outlined in previous year groups, in this case Year 4's addition and subtraction of fractions with the same denominator, and as such, so are the principles with which they must be approached. The mathematics may appear increasingly complex but they come from simple origins. Of course we expect our pupils to continue to develop their understanding of fractions as numbers, measures and operators by finding fractions of numbers and quantities but is this really any different from the learning that took place in Year 2? The complexity and required fluency perhaps but nothing has changed in terms of principles.

Counting continues ...

Pupils are expected to extend their counting from Year 4, using decimals and fractions including bridging zero, for example on a number line. What model and image have we been using to help us visualise the number line? The counting stick of course and as I've said before its use applies to fractions and decimals as much as it does to counting in integers in steps of 2, 5 and 10.

When pupils are saying, reading and writing decimal fractions and related tenths, hundredths and thousandths accurately and while being confident in checking the reasonableness of their answers to problems they can also refer to the counting stick but it is essential they are given opportunity to apply them to practical contexts. All of these requirements have been covered and you will often find they are minor tweaks from Years 3 and 4, which in themselves are tweaks of 1 and 2. The key is to understand why and how. Why do my pupils need to say, read and write decimal fractions? Sure the test in Year 6 may have a question asking pupils to write a fraction in words but is this the real reason? What use can it have in your children's lives, and this will naturally change depending on the context in which your school exists. Once you have worked out why you need to know how. If it is within your reach to recreate the conditions to apply the mathematics in the real world then I implore you to do so then to provide opportunity to investigate and explore in abstract contexts in order that the challenge should be maintained throughout the progression. Something as mundane as saying, reading and writing decimal fractions may have greater influence if you are prepared to look.

When pupils mentally add and subtract tenths, and 1-digit whole numbers and tenths they practise adding and subtracting decimals, including a mix of whole numbers and decimals, decimals with different numbers of decimal places, and complements of 1 (for example, 0.83 + 0.17 = 1). This is a direct link to the complements I have been promoting throughout the book. It simply requires an understanding of the key concepts. The foundations must be put in place of course. There is as little point in trying to bridge the gap between whole number complements and decimal complements if your pupils don't understand decimal place value as there is trying to use Dienes equipment to teach decimal place value if the pupils don't understand integer place value. If they are prepared and the steps have been put in place over time then pupils will have no trouble accessing and linking the concepts. If they haven't you will need to fill those gaps before you even consider such a notion.

Then, towards the end of the requirements in the fractions section for Year 5, they should go beyond the measurement and money models of decimals, for example, by solving puzzles involving decimals. I believe they will naturally make the link between percentages, fractions and decimals if their diet in problem solving has been rich and varied. Yet it is important to stress they must understand the concept of percentages coming from the concept of having 100 equal parts of something, hence the word cent (100) hidden in the middle of the word. In much the same way you introduced the concept of fractions draw direct links between the visual representation, the numerical representation and the fractional/decimal fraction equivalents. Make the links explicit and practical and you will build successfully on prior knowledge and understanding.

It may seem as if the mathematics is growing in stature and that pupils are required to access an ever broader range of subject knowledge but in all reality if the teaching and learning taking place throughout their education careers has been the best possible then the pupils are in a great position to take on even the most challenging of content. If not, you know by now you need to fill the gaps and then challenge.

Simply simplify?

This particular section appears to be one of the more complex in the National Curriculum and certainly an area which has had greater emphasis placed on it in recent years. When pupils are introduced to the need to *use common factors to simplify fractions; use common multiples to express fractions in the same denomination* they are required to apply their knowledge of multiplication. An understanding of commonality will allow them to access the concepts in the objective and provide a basis for any approach to them.

Comparing and ordering fractions

If we want pupils to *compare and order fractions, including those greater than one* we must take a similar approach as we did when the fractions were less than one. We must make the visual representation of the fractions clear and concise where necessary and there must be no doubt about the link between this image and the recorded figure. Fractional work like this can become quite abstract and so the greater relevance and meaning the greater the understanding on offer.

This objective can be approached through the use of the counting stick, particularly when ordering, and it can also be broached through use of the greater than and less than symbols, both of which we should be fairly familiar with at this stage. An understanding of the place value linked to the fractions is key and must be explicitly taught just as place value is throughout the curriculum. The principles already covered are clear, concise and mathematically accurate, meaning they are essential for pupil progress.

Pupils should practise, use and understand the addition and subtraction of fractions with different denominators by identifying equivalent fractions with the same denominator. They should start with fractions where the denominator of one fraction is a multiple of the other and progress to varied and increasingly complex problems. Here we can see once more the importance of a sound knowledge of the multiplication tables and the effect they can have on the curriculum. This is something that will be prevalent throughout the fractions guidance.

Proper fractions

A variety of images should be used to guide understanding when pupils are expected to *multiply simple pairs of proper fractions, writing the answer in its simplest form.* Building on the understanding of fractions from much earlier in the progression, pupils need to see the link between the written form of a fraction and the physical incarnation. It should be explicitly clear that the fractions must be equal parts of the one whole, e.g. thirds are three equal parts of one whole, and this should be your main aim when questioning pupils about their understanding. Pupils must be given the opportunity to realise that the equivalence of the size of each third, quarter or half is the very crux of the concept and that unequal fractions cannot even be considered thirds, quarters or halves at all. However you present the concept, which can even sometimes involve the delicious use of cakes, the equivalence must form the root of both your dialogue and questioning. There is a plethora of visual representations in a multitude of dimensions which can help aid the development of the concept of fractions and you can't really go wrong with any of them as long as you get the fundamental principles right.

Decimal association

In essence much of what is covered comes down to the introduction of mixed denominators and as long as pupils have a solid understanding of both multiplication and fractions the two can combine in the form of taught processes. Once the processes have been taught discretely, for instance *associating a fraction with division and calculating decimal fraction equivalents*, then pupils should be given the opportunity to apply this knowledge as widely and variedly as possible, drawing on all of the explanations and advice given throughout this book. The application of fractions to the curriculum can be seen in the final four requirements in Year 6 and as such the importance I have placed on problem solving and application of skills continues to hold the greatest value.

8 Ratio and proportion

Those of you in England will notice another 2014 revamp for the statutory requirements in Year 6 comes in the form of a separate ratio and proportion section which outlines an expectation that pupils learn to apply their knowledge of fractions, division and even place value, in fact almost everything they know with regards to abstract numerical concepts. Do not be alarmed, however, maths works best when in its simplest form and this shift in expectation is likely, once again, to give greater prominence to this key piece of understanding which is often confused and can be riddled by misconceptions. Keep everything clear and concise, understand the fundamentals you wish to put across and your pupils will access the learning inherent in the requirements without fail.

Relative size and missing values

For instance, pupils must *solve problems involving the relative sizes of two quantities where missing values can be found by using integer multiplication and division facts* and this, I must say, is one mouthful of a requirement. If we break it down, however, we can see that all we really have to do is understand the concept of ratio and proportion then fill in the blanks by applying our knowledge fluently. Right off the bat we must be clear that ratio describes the quantitative relationship between two amounts and essentially shows the number of times one value contains or is contained within the other while proportion refers to a part, share, or number considered in comparative relation to a whole. The difference, while one of the more subtle we encounter at the primary level, has no doubt troubled practitioners and children alike globally and I would highly recommend you make it a priority to master before you try to disseminate across the masses.

Creative mathematicians

Creating their own word problems and the associated models and images can be a sign of understanding at greater depth. Choosing which pieces of information to include, which to omit, and giving a considered rationale for each decision is a sign of true mathematical fluency.

To deliver this particular concept with the desired accuracy you must establish the vocabulary you intend to use. The ratio is the association between two or more quantities. The ratio 3:2 recognises the associated rate of 3 for every 2 e.g. 3 metres for every 2 minutes. Ratios can be equivalent and sometimes you can refer to the above ratio as 3 to 2. I personally would stick to the use of 3 for every 2 until the pupils are secure in their understanding. It is imperative you explore the terms association, quantities, equivalence and the phrase 'for every'. If you do this you will have started to lay the foundations of a solid understanding of ratio and proportion. Sometimes it is worth presenting misconceptions as your own ideas, we should be modelling how we deal with such occurrences after all, and perhaps you could record a ratio as a fraction. Do the children notice? Can you address it with the explanation given above or similar? I would suggest yes and implore you to do so. The same principle can be applied when *solving problems involving similar shapes where the scale factor is known or can be found,* although they will likely be working with measurements in a context that is less than clear.

Juice?

For me, the best way to make this learning relevant and meaningful is through the use of investigative strategies outlined in an earlier section. I've seen many teachers create a smoothie making challenge where pupils must find the perfect ratio of fruit to create the most delicious smoothie. As such the ratio of all manner of fruit must be taken into account, not to mention the eventual marketing and selling of the smoothies which could be a tour de force of real life maths in itself.

You may alternatively wish to use a squash/juice to water ratio or the soup/puree equivalent but whatever the final decision may be, the principles remain the same and the mathematics must be the focus. It is easy to become distracted by the activity and engagement levels and in turn allow mathematical accuracy to slip. This must never be the case and the mathematical language and concepts must be your top priority throughout any sequence of lessons.

When teaching pupils to *solve problems involving the calculation of percentages and the use of percentages for comparison* we need only teach our pupils that to find a given percentage we simply divide the numerator by the denominator e.g. $\frac{15}{30}$ would be $15 \div 30$ which gives an answer of 0.5. We then multiply the decimal by 100 to find our percentage. $0.5 \times 100 = 50$ so our answer must be 50%. In all honesty it takes quite a bit of fluency to use this particular method without the use of a calculator, and in the real world you would largely have such supporting materials at hand; however, as English pupils will have no such assistance at the end of Key Stage 2 it is worth considering the methods on offer and how we can best marry their understanding of a range of mathematical concepts in order that they meet the expected standard.

The marriage of fractions, decimals and percentages

Without the use of percentages for comparison this requirement becomes a reference solely to the ability to calculate percentages, which of course we know it is not. In turn I believe the use of role-play to deepen understanding is quite fitting. Providing pupils with price tags, I would ask them to organise a shopping experience where a range of deals are on offer. The only caveat? The discounts must be presented in terms of fractions, decimals and percentages off. The shoppers will then be forced to choose the best deals based on their understanding of which discounts provide the greatest savings. An investigation such as this will lend itself to any cross-curricular situation and can be altered relatively easily to suit a range of developmental levels/access points.

Eventually pupils must *solve problems involving unequal sharing and grouping using knowledge of fractions and multiples* which boils down to pupils having to solve problems involving unequal quantities. The guidance says they form the foundation for later formal approaches to ratio and proportion and as such should be treated as a key aspect of the 2014 National Curriculum. In real terms all our pupils must truly know and understand is that the concept of ratio will be applied to our knowledge of fractions and vice versa in order that their true relevance and use can be garnered. It is not my intention to oversimplify here but rather highlight the key understanding for you to focus your efforts on when providing opportunities for your pupils to act and reason fluently and confidently.

Simplest form

When fostering the application and problem solving skills associated with this particular statutory requirement there is a lot to be said for the traditional problems we may have encountered ourselves as children, whereby a range of objects are on offer and the ratio must be garnered from this most visual of representation.

Once they have calculated the ratio we must then challenge them to provide the ratio in its lowest terms (the ratio and proportion equivalent of simplifying). For if they can they will have mastered the skills necessary to meet the requirement and be ready to apply their knowledge to whatever situation you may deem suitable.

This may take the form of some building work, gardening, recycling or painting, as long as pupils can apply this key and often abstract concept in a practical context.

And while this often most complex of concepts can appear daunting for pupils and practitioners alike, I do believe the explanations above serve to relieve some of the pressure and can even act as an entry point for the development of greater understanding for all. If nothing else keep it simple and make the concepts explicit. If the rest of the curriculum has been delivered in a meaningful way then pupils will have no choice but to apply their knowledge with the desired confidence, fluency and control.

Pie chart starting point

The way in which problems involving ratio and proportion are worded can be key to providing opportunities for pupils to reach a greater depth of understanding, as can asking pupils to reason about whether or not they would use the same methods as the person in a given example. However, that being said, there are few examples more self-explanatory in nature than the use of a pie chart and one given piece of information to challenge the most able in their understanding of the fundamental principles.

If we ask them to estimate the quantity represented by each of the other pieces of the pie then from this starting point they will have to estimate the relative value of the other slices, calculate the ratio before ultimately estimating the answer to whatever question was posed in the first place.

9 Measurement

With instruction to compare, describe and solve practical problems through the use of measurement, the clear focus on the language of measurement to be used in English Year 1 classes is evidence of the expectations for practitioners working with children in this year group and throughout the entire primary phase. Going a long way to vindicating my approach to linguistic consistency, the English National Curriculum makes clear the difference between a range of measures and the language used to describe them. You must be aware, however, that while terms are used interchangeably, this will not definitely remain the case beyond this particular stage of development and a precise understanding of where the pupils are going to is necessary even for those working with the youngest of our primary pupils.

Vocabulary is key

The description of length, for instance, explicitly encourages the use of *long and short, longer and shorter, tall and short* and *double and half* in the formative years of primary mathematics. I would compel you and your colleagues to ensure that any explanations of the vocabulary remain clear and precise in order that you create a clear stance towards the language of comparison. As I have said before the assimilation of language is an ongoing process which must begin as early as possible if sufficient time is to be given to the process.

If you are consistent in your approach and the same can be said of your colleagues then you are half way to creating the perfect conditions for accelerated, deepened and meaningful progress. When we consider mass and weight we must be clear on our use of *heavy and light, heavier than* and *lighter than*. Capacity and volume - *full/empty, more than, less than, half, half full, quarter*. Time - *quicker, slower, earlier and later*. The language is clear for all to see so it should be relatively simple to put into effect, leaving you with more time to focus on ways to make the mathematics relevant and meaningful to the pupils in your care.

If you focus your efforts in this way then not only will your pupils be more confident in their reasoning but they will be significantly more succinct as well, something which will lead to greater mathematical accuracy and understanding for all involved. You may be tempted to use some of these words to describe the relative size or comparison of numbers but be warned that the technical terms given here refer directly to measures rather than the place or face value of numbers and should be treated as such. To use them accurately is to use them in the way they were intended and to leave greater and less to act as numerical descriptors. This in itself is key to maintaining the clarity we are all striving to attain.

When it actually comes time to *begin to measure and record lengths and heights, mass/ weight, capacity and volume and time* pupils will be so engrained in the use of the correct and accurate language that they will have a much greater understanding of the concepts they are applying practically. This secure grounding will allow subsequent teachers to build on the irrefutable understanding of the pupils in question, meaning measure in Year 1 can act as a precursor for true depth of challenge in Years 2, 3 and beyond. This leaves us time to consider how often measure is allowed to take on a similar guise regardless of which year group it is being taught in. *(Much like when instruction texts created by Year 1 pupils differ very little from those created in Year 3.)*

Strategies

Pupils must devise their own strategies for problem solving within the various aspects of measurement and when we consider greater depth of understanding there is a suggestion that it could involve the way problems are presented in many cases.

For instance imagine we have a balanced scale with a teddy bear on one end and four compare bears on the other end. We could give the weight of the teddy bear and ask pupils to devise the weight of each compare bear.

Simple perhaps but certainly an example of how the presentation of a problem can drastically alter pupil cognition and encourage them to think in a more lateral and creative fashion.

Whether this is a notion you are considering for the first time or something which sounds all too familiar, we must work to ensure it is prevented and that clear and accurate differentiation are encouraged at all costs. I fully believe this is something which should certainly go without saying but similar instances are so frequent that it really must be said again, again and again until it resonates sufficiently with the masses. If the grounding and vocabulary is secure, as we have discussed, then the level of challenge can be driven to much deeper levels than we ever thought possible. It is clear that this responsibility, in the formal sense of the National Curriculum, lies initially with the Year 1 teacher but can begin in Nursery and last all the way to Year 6 and beyond.

Measuring across the curriculum, time and space

If the messages in the preceding chapters have meant as much to you as they do to me then it should be clear by this stage that 'measures' is the perfect topic in which to harness the power of real life experiences in order to create lasting and meaningful mathematical connections.

I would suggest you double up by teaching direct skills through the application of the mathematical concepts in this chapter. For instance, you may wish to teach the addition of 3-digit numbers, and where better to get your examples/questions than by working with measuring cylinders full, or not so full, of water.

Similarly if you want to extend the understanding of your pupils you may wish to explore the history of measurement, asking pupils to devise a rationale for their own or an ancient system of measurement. The Romans, Greeks, Egyptians, or almost any ancient civilisation for that matter, will have used some method of measuring and had often had ingenious reasons for doing so. All that is left is for your pupils to consider the fundamental principles of measurement and to explain them as succinctly and accurately as is humanly possible.

Humanly possible?

Extra-terrestrial measurements, now there's a thought, how fast does light travel again, 299,792,458 metres per second – that could definitely be turned into an investigation requiring the application of some serious mathematical understanding!

Standard units

When pupils are learning to *choose and use appropriate standard units to estimate and measure length/height, mass, temperature and capacity to the nearest unit* it is imperative the vocabulary of measurement is accurate and concise. This almost goes without saying as the accuracy of the measurement clearly relies on the standardisation of the units of measurement. The metrics in question – *metres, centimetres, kilograms, grams, litres and millilitres* – are all standard units of measurement recognised in the United Kingdom and are mostly members of the metric system itself.

While the officially recognised system in the UK is the system of imperial measurement which includes miles and pints, eventually pupils will have to draw comparisons between the two systems because, as expected, they are to be fully confident in their use of measure by the time they come to learn to *measure, compare, add and subtract: lengths (m/cm/ mm); mass (kg/g); volume/capacity (l/m)*. That is not to say that they must be fluent in their application when they begin to choose and use standard units but rather is an indication of what will naturally follow.

The foundations, for me, however, are much more easily accessible in the metric system than its imperial counterpart and it is infinitely more intuitive for young children to continue to work in the understanding that place value gets 10, 100, 1,000 times greater than to begin researching the origins of the 1824 Weights and Measures Act. Pupils in Year 2 are consolidating their understanding of base 10 and really don't need to be confused by the reasons there are 568ml in a pint. Instead they are expected to, and should, use their time to conserve prior concepts and understanding, for example, adding and subtracting lengths in much the same way they would add and subtract anything else.

A role to play

Hopefully weights and measures will have had a role to play in the formation of pupils' understanding of the concepts such as addition and subtraction but if they have not then you have the perfect opportunity, or statutory responsibility, to do so. One would expect the use of the formal written algorithms, perhaps even the introduction of decimalisation at times, though not statutorily, and always the growth of our understanding of the relationship between the measures in order that the concepts move freely and securely between abstract, pictorial and concrete. The use of decimalisation, linked with fractions and with place value, weighs heavily on the requirement relating to money as pupils are expected to *estimate, compare and calculate different measures, including money in pounds and pence* which really shouldn't be anything overly new to the pupils and perhaps just an opportunity to contextualise previous or related learning.

You must, however, take time to explain the origins of the prefixes in use in the metric system because the role they play is key in the development of true and efficient understanding. Kilo, cent and mill each hide clues to the original meaning they held in their language of origin, whether it be Greek, Latin or even French and this information will become extremely useful during the later comparison as the history of weights and measures becomes apparent, but for now the foundations can be laid at the same time as understanding is promoted.

Conversions

Once these foundations have been laid pupils must begin to *convert between different units of measure (for example, kilometre to metre; hour to minute)* which realistically just incorporates everything we have learned in previous years. Relatively little discrete teaching will be needed if the relationships have been allowed to grow and if understanding of the concepts is relational. If a pupil has a mere habitual understanding of the concepts then you will need to go back and plug the gaps in order to create a more rounded view of the relationship between the given measures. We haven't even begun to consider the difference between metric and imperial but you can guarantee this will feature in Year 5. As I have said before the metric system works in the same way our base 10 place value system works and should, eventually, become intuitive to our pupils. Where misconceptions or a lack of understanding does arise you must ask pupils to model their problem solving skills and then from these conversations draw out the learning which needs to take place.

We haven't even been asked to consider the difference between metric and imperial before now but, as warned, by the time pupils reach Year 5 when we ask them to *understand and use approximate equivalences between metric units and common imperial units such as inches, pounds and pints,* the expectation is finally on the table. Here the history of measurement, the origins of the metric system in revolutionary Europe and all that is encompassed by the different measurements can be drawn out. It is more than simple recitation and multiplication by 1.6 or 0.6, it is an understanding of a state of mind and our shared global culture. It is my understanding that during the French Revolution of 1789, the architects and eventual victors on the Republican side decided the imperial system of measures and weights was a sore reminder of all the injustice that had gone before and so the metric system was introduced.

You may even want to set this up as an exercise for your pupils where they check the validity of this interpretation of events. Can they verify the actual inception of the metric system? It may serve a double purpose and reinforce the importance of accuracy and the use of source material, something which I fear has gone by the wayside in the technological age.

Work smarter not harder

You won't necessarily have the time or capacity to mentally multiply by 1.6 or 0.6 but help is at hand because there are alternative solutions.

Take the number of kilometres, halve it, quarter that and add the two together to get the equivalent number of miles e.g. (64 km = 32 + 8 = 40 miles).

When working in the other direction simply take the number of miles, divide by 5 and multiply by 8 to find the equivalent number of kilometres e.g. (40 ÷ 5 = 8 × 8 = 64 km).

Money, money, money

A small but nonetheless important note, pardon the pun, regarding *knowing the value of different denominations of coins and notes* refers to the fact that children should always, and I mean always, be given the opportunity to use real money when learning about money. By all means put systems in place to protect your investment but plastic coins and fake bank notes have no place in the primary classroom. Nor any classroom for that matter! All children must be taught the true value of the currency and this can only be done with legal tender itself. We cannot expect them to have any respect for faux currency and nor should we.

If they have been given sufficient opportunity to explore money at home and in school then pupils will have less difficulty grasping the concept inherent in the *recognition and use of symbols for pounds (£) and pence (p); combining amounts to make a particular value.* This should be the stuff of everyday life, yet the digital age has snatched a vital life skill from our pupils. Unless you can set up PayPal within your classroom I would suggest you ensure role-play and an actual educational visit to the supermarket are included in your planning around this particular requirement. It should be second nature to take part in such transactions but such has the nature of economic experience changed it is very unlikely to be so any more. Pupils who work with money on a regular basis don't record £5.09p because they know and they understand, they have a deeper sense of the concept. To prevent you must allow them to experience.

Keep the change

One of the requirements is that pupils *find different combinations of coins that equal the same amounts of money.* A fool proof example of how role-play can be used to develop concepts and prevent misconceptions in itself and the perfect opportunity to allow them to *solve problems in a practical context involving addition and subtraction of money of the same unit, including* (and here's the kicker) *giving change.* Is there any reason why they can't actually be engaged in genuine exchanges of money, with appropriate supervision, in a constant and worthwhile homage to ECM5 (Every Child Matters 5), economic wellbeing? This is the most sure fire way to ensure they understand money. Make it real. You aren't flippant with your own money and you'll soon work hard to make sure you've recorded your earnings correctly if you make even the slightest mistake. It requires planning but it is worth it to instil both the literal and cultural value of money in their long term memories and deeper still. This concept can also be applied to the *addition and subtraction of amounts of money when giving change, using both £ and p in practical contexts.*

The requirements explain that they must *give change* and again I highly recommend they are engaged in genuine exchanges of money. Make it real with appropriate supervision, in a constant and worthwhile homage to ECM5 (Every Child Matters 5), economic wellbeing. This is the most sure fire way to ensure they understand money. Make it real. You aren't flippant with your own money and you'll soon work hard to make sure you've recorded your earnings correctly if you make even the slightest mistake. It requires planning but it is worth the hard work to instil both the literal and cultural value of money in the long term memories of our pupils.

The apprentice – KS2 edition

Perhaps an enterprise week where pupils start a business, cake stall, decorative tiles manufacturer, whatever they can imagine and create, and donate the money they raise at an end of the week sale to charity. You may not want to settle for a week and have an ongoing commitment to economic development and understanding. The power to do so is in the hands of you and your pupils no matter how young and those first steps are waiting to be taken.

Chronological sequencing

When expecting pupils to *sequence events in chronological order* it actually says *using language* in the requirement itself and while they may be 'examples' you'd be foolhardy to ignore this stepping stone towards a greater understanding of how we measure time. Practical activities such as the creation of a video or a book based on daily routines will allow you to draw *before and after, first, today, yesterday, tomorrow, morning, afternoon and evening* in a natural and meaningful way. Here the importance lies in making these almost random and seemingly abstract concepts concrete. What does yesterday really mean? Consider all the possible ways you can show someone how something comes before or after something else. This must be practical, engaging but most importantly relevant. This mathematics must be entrenched in first-hand experience so that the concept can hook onto the event and grow in unison with the memory.

What day is it?

The days of the week and months of the year are mentioned in Year 1, yet in my experience there are many examples of Year 3 children in existence without this knowledge. Perhaps this is a clear example of the hike in expectation or an agenda of the architects of the 2014 National Curriculum but either way, daily reference to the date, season and their position in our calendar with reference to next and last are sure fire ways to establish an understanding of this important knowledge. It is, however, not enough just to do so. There must be some discrete teaching followed up by the rehearsal, conversation and daily application.

Decimalisation of time

You may want to consider the use of decimalisation to describe periods of time as a way to foster greater depth of understanding. Ask your pupils to explain the answers to the following questions. How many hours would 4.8 days be? What would 3.6 hours be in hours and minutes? Give them possible answers – selecting the most common misconceptions of course – and ask them to reason fluently about their decisions.

The same must be said of the time, an area of knowledge many children go without for too long, as it must be addressed both discretely and holistically. It does, however, present us with one of the all-time classic misconceptions introduced by adults – the big and small hand. Be very, very careful that the language you use is mathematically accurate for it may be, and often is, too late to undo once the pupils are in lower Key Stage 2. The shortest hand on the clock is known as the hour hand because it designates the upcoming or previous hour. The longest hand on the clock is known as the minute hand because it designates the current minute. Often there is a third, equally long but considerably thinner hand, known as the second hand. This does not mean second in terms of ordinance but rather works to designate the precise second to be shown on the clock. Refer, by all means, to them as the hour or short hand, minute or long hand and thin or second hand but do not call them the big and small hand. It is neither big nor clever and you won't do yourself any favours. As with all of the vocabulary involved in this most formative of year groups the earlier they start the earlier they grasp and the deeper they understand.

What time is it again?

When telling the time, particularly upon the introduction of *telling and writing the time to five minutes, including quarter past/to the hour … and showing these times* we must, as we have said, be careful to use the correct terminology to describe each of the hands. The difference between the expectation at Year 1 and Year 2 is the ability to show the time and here we must be careful to give an accurate portrayal of our time keeping devices. You'll notice that on most, if not all clocks, the hands often fill a space between the different numbers, signifying the distance to the next or from the previous hour. It is important that this message comes across to the pupils. Their clocks, no matter how young pupils are, will never be accurate if they are encouraged to portray inaccurate representations of time.

You can encourage them to *know the number of minutes in an hour and the number of hours in a day* with continual reinforcement, much like the days of the week and months of the year. They are facts they need to learn. Facts which we use every day of our lives and can apply each and every day. What is important is that we can both tell and represent the time accurately. We must understand the very nuances of the clock and we do this through an insistence on accuracy. Draw the clock as you mean it to be read. That will prevent most, if not all, misconceptions relating to this particular statutory requirement. Of course, all clocks may eventually become digitised and this knowledge superfluous, but until then we must endure and insist that it is one tradition that does not go the way of the dinosaurs.

Telling the time takes an interesting twist in Year 3 because not only are they expected to *tell and write the time from an analogue clock* (as if they exist outside of museums) but it is also set to include *Roman numerals from I to XII, and 12-hour and 24-hour clocks*. Pupils at this point should no longer need to be reminded of the correct terminology to describe each of the hands if they have had the proper linguistic diet in the previous two years.

Ante meridiem

Of course by this stage any reading of the clock should be down to the finest minutiae as we have already passed the point of 5 minute intervals in Year 2. Now, no matter what appears on the clock, be it an X, I or even a VIII, your pupils should be able to read whatever time you throw at them. Not only that, but they should be able to convert between 24 and 12 hour variances should they decide to travel to Central Europe on a whim. In terms of the acquisition of technical skills of value, the pupils must know that the hour hand makes two full rotations of the clock in a day, thus the numbers on an analogue clock represent two times of day. Key vocabulary includes ante meridiem and post meridiem, not ante meridian as it is sometimes mistakenly known, which literally translate from Latin as before midday and after midday. Straightforward enough and a good enough explanation for your pupils.

This understanding that the hour hand makes two full rotations in a day is inextricably linked to process of *knowing the number of seconds in a minute* if not *the number of days in each month, year and leap year* as well. To know that the clock is an amalgamation of 60s is almost the final page in the time keeper's manual. One full turn of the second hand, 60 seconds and one full turn of the minute hand, 60 minutes. Where this picture goes a bit awry is when we get into one full turn of the hour hand and end up with 12 hours instead of 60. That is, however, because of the 365.25 day elliptical orbit of a planet tilted on its axis by 23 degrees and turning at 20,000 kilometres per hour to make one full rotation every 24 hours during its journey around the Sun. Of course, all the information you will ever need to share with your Year 3 pupils is contained within this sentence but this is not the case for every celestial body.

Celestial investigations

You may also wish to share the fact that Venus, while similar in size to planet Earth, rotates in the opposite direction from our home in the solar system and a day there takes longer than a year. This is definitely something you will want your pupils to investigate, perhaps even with less specificity and a greater emphasis on generalisations being drawn by the behaviour of planet Earth. Put your students in control of their own learning and see where you end up.

You may ask where they will get the time to fit in the *comparison of durations of events (for example to calculate the time taken by particular events or tasks)* but this could, and should, be part of your everyday experiences in school. Eventually they will be asked to consider and describe time durations over the hour so it is probably worth introducing the line shown in Figure 9.1 as an example of things to come and a method of recording durations of time.

03:00_____03:10_____03:40

(+10mins)   (+30mins)

Figure 9.1

Digital and 24 hour time

Following a curved ascent into Year 3, the fundamentals of telling the time continues on a lateral tangent in Year 4 with pupils now expected to read *digital 12- and 24-hour clocks*. Pupils at this point should no longer need to be reminded of the correct terminology to describe each of the hands, not only because they should have had the proper linguistic diet in the previous three years but because the digitalisation of the clock face removes the need for the hands at all. Now, no matter what appears on the clock, your pupils should be able to read whatever time you throw at them in the 12 and 24 hour analogue and digital versions. At the risk of over simplifying it I believe your pupils need to know how to tell the difference between times and they need to be able to describe the time. Opportunities to read a range of clocks on a daily basis should take care of this and targeted questioning can effectively support pupil progress. If you don't have a range of clocks in the room use the technology on offer to present the time in different ways throughout the day. This will be the most meaningful method of supporting the learning process.

Further to this, pupils are now expected to be able to *solve problems involving converting from hours to minutes; minutes to seconds; years to months; weeks to days* and if they have been given the proper diet and know their times tables, particularly their six and seven times, then they will be well on the way to being able to solve these problems. The key to preventing misconceptions here is the insistence on the use of the correct unit of measurement. To convert hours to minutes we multiply by 60, while the reverse is true of converting minutes to hours, here we divide by 60. A proper understanding of place value and multiplication, as outlined already in the curriculum, will prepare for such instances. The same can be said of minutes to seconds and vice versa. To convert between years to months we multiply by 12 and weeks to days we multiply by 7. All very straightforward, yet pupils are eager to record the original unit of measurement. This must not be allowed to complicate such simple and straightforward procedures.

Our pupils need to *solve problems involving converting between units of time* and *use all four operations to solve problems involving measure using decimal notation and scaling* and while it could appear as though these expectations are raised, again they build on everything that has gone before them. It may seem by now as if I am a major proponent of the 2014 curriculum but this is not necessarily the case. I simply see the benefit in what we have in front of us and have come to terms with how I would approach the teaching of mathematics across Key Stage 1 and Key Stage 2. If pupils have accessed the curriculum in the right way and at the right breadth and depth then they will be able to access even the most upper echelons of the expectations. Apply the principles of previous year groups, apply them consistently and your pupils will grow into the mathematicians they can become. Of this I am certain.

Rectilinear?

Although progression in money has gone by the wayside by this point and it has been sucked into the black hole that is the application of decimal place value, *measure and calculate the perimeter of a rectilinear figure (including squares) in centimetres and metres* comes in to fill the void which remains. Rectilinear refers to shapes whose edges meet at right angles. This encompasses both compound and regular polygons so we should be wary just to define rectilinear as squares and rectangles. Any shape, the cruciform for instance, where the angles meet at right angles can be considered a suitable candidate. This hikes up the complexity of the objective no end when considered in this light, however the true challenge lies in the description of the formula for calculating the perimeter of rectilinear quadrilaterals where the formula can be described as $2(a + b)$. Naturally you would spend your time providing opportunities for pupils to describe the formula in words, e.g. *we add the two lengths then we add the two widths before adding them all together to find the total perimeter*, then take each expression of the formula and work it towards the simplified formula presented above.

It is worth remembering to remind the pupils that the perimeter is the distance around the outside of a shape and the area is the space covered by a two-dimensional shape. In Year 4 pupils are allowed to *find the area of rectilinear shapes by counting squares*, presumably covering a particular space. In our quest to consolidate this concept we must be careful not to provide opportunity for misconception through the resources we provide. If we are talking about square centimetres then we must provide centimetre squared paper and be sure the paper is in fact what we say it is. If we are to use alternative sized paper then know the exact dimensions or don't use them in your explanations and dialogues. Square metres should be metres squared unless you plan on teaching scale which I wouldn't recommend at present. Be one hundred per cent sure the resources you plan to use are conducive to accurate learning and while it may take a little extra effort it will be worth it in the end. If not for you, then certainly for the pupils in your care.

Area and perimeter

There are many examples of investigations which can be used to extend and deepen pupil understanding of area and perimeter but none as straightforward as the following statement:

> Dan draws two rectangles and the second has a greater perimeter than the first. Dan says the second rectangle will also have a greater area. Is Dan correct? Explain your reasoning.

As pupils progress towards complete mastery of area and perimeter they must eventually learn to *measure and calculate the perimeter of composite rectilinear shapes in centimetres and metres* which again seems to have filled the void left by knowledge and understanding of money, though this isn't a point I want to labour. The use of standard units such as centimetres squared and metres squared is formalised here as is the estimation of irregular shapes. I, however, recommended this be broached earlier in order to challenge pupils and if you ensure the relative size, as exemplified in resources with actual centimetre squared paper, is handed down then you will have provided a base or sturdy foundations on which pupils, and successive teachers alike, can build.

Convinced?

When working with this particular content area I highly recommend giving your pupils possible solutions to a composite shape problem (with reasoning or calculations which show the thought process) and ask them if they are convinced by what they read. Essentially they are taking their understanding to the next level by acting in role as someone who is assessing learning and will be required to maximise the use of their understanding in the process.

Unit conversion

Back on familiar ground now pupils must *solve problems involving the calculation and conversion of units of measure, using decimal notation up to three decimal places where appropriate* and again we must ensure they are consistently applying decimal place value which, although not mentioned in the statutory guidance, is littered throughout the National Curriculum. At this point the conversion is within base 10 and should be intuitive for pupils. A sound understanding of place value as outlined in prior chapters will see your pupils through this potentially challenging terrain relatively unscathed.

When teaching pupils to convert between miles and kilometres you must consider the history as outlined in Year 5 but really you must ensure your pupils remember that there are 1.6 kilometres in 1 mile and 0.6 miles in 1 kilometre. There are actually 1.60934 kilometres for every mile and 0.621371 miles for every 1 kilometre but it is your prerogative how much detail you ascribe. Much of the real life application has been removed by technological advancements but it is an important skill nevertheless. A little earlier we spoke about working smarter rather than harder and again these suggestions remain relevant here and can be used to enhance efficiency as long as pupils are clear in their understanding of the key concepts and fundamental principles involved.

Pupils who recognise that shapes with the same areas can have different perimeters and vice versa are pupils who have explored and investigated shape in a manner befitting primary education. It is an understanding which comes through experience and cannot be taught because it has little to no grounding unless it has been investigated.

Formulae

When calculating the area of parallelograms and triangles you must remember that the formula for the area of a parallelogram can be algebraically described as a = bh or area =

base x height whereas triangles can be calculated by halving the base and multiplying by the height. Simple, straightforward and to the point. Once pupils see this you can then open up the possibility that they create their own descriptions of the relationships and rules they encounter. I personally would encourage pupils to do so throughout their careers and move from the use of words to describe to the use of symbols to describe the formulae as their understanding progressed. Newton's second law of motion, or $\vec{F} = m\vec{a}$ to the classical physicists among you, is another great example you can make practical. Simply it says that the force on an object is equal to the mass x action (the action being the push you give to a ball for instance) and while pupils may not be able to work with this in real terms they can certainly be shown how the value of something can be described by a single letter.

Measurement as a concept forms a large part of the maths we use in our daily lives and as such should be treated with the importance it deserves. I strongly urge you to consider how you and your colleagues can make this particular aspect of mathematical learning meaningful, engaging and relevant for our pupils, while continually aiming to create the strongest connections possible between the various concepts. Be aware of the role-play opportunities and tailor them to the specific needs of your pupils and you will have taken a significant step towards the provision of high quality first-hand experiences. This in turn will lead to high quality dialogue, the reinforcement of key concepts and exceptional progress on the part of your pupils. Perfect!

10 Geometry - properties of shape

It is no surprise that where pupils should be *taught to name common 2-D and 3-D shapes* we find direct reference to the orientation and sizes of shapes. As we have discussed, pupils should be no more led to believe a triangle has a top or bottom than they should be given 3 dimensional representations of 2-D shapes without utter clarification as to the nature of the resource's use. The importance of labelling of such resources correctly cannot be overstated. Call them *3 dimensional representations of 2 dimensional shapes*, *3-D shapes*, *3 dimensional shapes*, call them all of the above but please do not actively seek to immerse children in an inaccurate environment with incorrect vocabulary which will only have a lasting effect on their concept development for years to come. I implore you to actively seek out such inaccuracies and make it your mission to ensure the environment provided by you and your colleagues is second to none in terms of mathematical accuracy.

Top trumps

The creation and use of a set of trump cards may provide the perfect opportunity for pupils to consider the properties of the shapes relevant to their year group in a context which places great value on such properties. They will, I assume, be familiar with the more traditional versions of the game whereby cars or superheroes are pitted against each other in an age old battle of wit and guile.

The real challenge for the pupils will be to create a context in which the comparison of shapes is as interesting as the games actually made by the toy companies. All the while remaining mathematically accurate and challenging the understanding of their peers.

Might be worth looking into the marketing of such a product since they've gone to all that trouble.

A lot has been said about shape already and I have called for action to ensure it is not a case of general knowledge relating to shape names and properties because it is my aim that this particular content area is given the respect it is entitled to and allowed to thrive as a key area of the use and application of mathematics. When pupils are taught to *identify and describe the properties of 2-D shapes, including the number of sides and line symmetry in a vertical line* this can, as previously mentioned, become a matter of general knowledge, all easily recorded in a table and likely to be tested through just such a table or a Venn or Carroll diagram. It, however, should not be the be all and end all of your foray into shape, no matter what year group you currently teach. Your responsibility is to ensure the depth and breadth of the curriculum is unsurpassed and that pupils are able to manipulate and apply knowledge with fluency. To do so they will have to have been taught to question and they will have to have been given a varied and rich diet of opportunity which would indeed include the exploration of 2-D shapes but would not be limited to the literal identification of the number of sides. This is an important skill at this stage, no doubt, but it does not summarise the entirety of the expectations of the curriculum. Remember, if our pupils are to achieve an age appropriate standard then they must be able to apply their knowledge and if they are to achieve 'mastery' (though the definition of this is likely to remain indefinitely undecided) the opportunities for application must grow increasingly abstract in context.

Isometric challenge

A variety of challenges pertaining to the representation of shapes can be accessed through the use of isometric paper. You may wish to alter their arrangement on the paper, create a range of polygons or even devise nets of 3-D shapes. Whatever you choose the use of this particular type of paper will force pupils to create a mental construct and use it to provide a pictorial representation. It will also provide opportunity for greater accuracy and the creation of both 2-D and 3-D representations.

That being said, before you can extend the depth of pupil engagement and understanding there is a need to learn the basics, before they can be applied. Every architect from Alvar Aalto to Alexander Yusuf has had to start with the foundations and we as facilitators of learning are no different. The basics which feature in the Year 2 properties of shape section of the 2014 National Curriculum focus largely on the identification and description of the properties of 2-D shapes, 3-D shapes and the identification of 2-D shapes on the surface of 3-D shapes mixed in with a comparison, typically the aforementioned Venn and Carroll diagram exercises I'm sure you are all familiar with, for good health. It is your choice how you wish to deliver and if you wish to accept the call to inspire through shape. NCETM (www.ncetm.org.uk) and NRICH Maths (www.nrich.maths.org) are excellent examples of places to visit when in need of inspiration in this area which will allow me to focus on the use of language. There is even, as we come to terms with the necessity for greater clarity and organisation, a document which links the nrich.org investigations to the National Curriculum objectives. Five to ten years ago this was unheard of and NRICH was only really explored and tamed by the specialist or the dedicated. Now, however, things really couldn't be simpler if you are prepared to take the time to look.

Glossary of terms

At this point I feel a glossary of terms mid-section suits our needs most effectively. Ensure you understand them and can use them consistently correctly and you will provide pupils with the basis to explore in the way in which you truly desire but never thought possible.

- *Corner* - the point where two or more edges or sides meet.
- *Edge* - the line along which two faces meet.
- *Face* - the flat surface of a solid shape e.g. a cuboid has six faces.
- *Flat* - a level surface with no depth.
- *Shape* - form or outline.
- *Side* - a straight line joining the vertices of a polygon.
- *Symmetry* - an object is symmetrical when one half is a mirror image of the other.
- *Vertex/Vertices* - a point where two or more rays or the arms of an angle meet, the adjacent sides of a polygon meet, or the edges of a solid figure meet.
- *Vertical* - at right angles to the horizon.

The words selected have been because they are specifically mentioned in the 2014 National Curriculum and as such are statutory for teachers in England. This does not diminish their mathematical importance. Their use is of vital importance and should be treated as such in the way in which they are approached in the classroom. When unsure about the meaning of a word don't use it frivolously; there are many great examples of mathematics dictionaries which can be used to prevent misconceptions thriving in an inaccurate metaphorical breeding ground. This brief glossary will grow as the curriculum demands it but for now the children of Year 2 need to know what they are, what they mean and what this means in 'the real world'. What does it mean to them? What should it mean? Is it conducive to understanding the mathematics inherent in the concept?

The properties of shape section of the Year 4 curriculum sees the introduction of new vocabulary which must be disseminated with accuracy, enthusiasm and aplomb. Pupils are now expected to describe:

- *Acute angle* - less than 90 degrees.
- *Equilateral* - having all three angles and sides equal, a congruent 60 degrees to be precise.
- *Irregular* - not even or balanced in shape or arrangement.
- *Isosceles* - having two sides of equal length, and as a result two angles.
- *Obtuse angle* - greater than 90 degrees, less than 180 degrees.
- *Quadrilateral* - four-sided 2-D shape, though they probably already know this.
- *Regular* - arranged in or constituting a constant or definite pattern.
- *Right angle* - 90 degrees exactly.
- *Scalene* - having sides unequal in length.
- *Symmetry* - agreement in dimensions, due proportion and arrangement where the image is balanced on both sides.
- *Triangle* - a three-sided shape with internal angles of 180 degrees.

As such the words above will encompass the learning inherent in the Year 4 objectives and build on the learning which took place in Years 2 and 3. You will be able to see that through knowledge of this key vocabulary they will be able to *compare and classify geometric shapes, including quadrilaterals and triangles, based on their properties and sizes* while also *identifying acute and obtuse angles and comparing and ordering angles up to two right angles by size*. The concepts are the embodiment of the language. If pupils understand the language they will understand the concepts.

An unexpected turn

Alas, the properties of shape takes an unexpected turn in Year 3 and while it continues to build a little on the descriptions of shape developed in Year 2 it feels as if they are biding their time. You should, however, not need to worry about this because if they can apply their knowledge from Year 2 then they will be well equipped once you teach them to *draw 2-D shapes and make 3-D shapes using modelling materials*, to *recognise them in different orientations and describe them*. The key here is the description. This is nothing new and for me doesn't really build on the previous year's learning. You could certainly refer to the mini-glossary in Year 2 to describe the shapes as there is nothing new to add but be wary that the non-statutory guidance identifies the need to extend this understanding to non-symmetrical polygons and polyhedrons. I'm not entirely sure why this isn't statutory but it feeds into our ideas about shapes never being *upside down* and really what you need to do is ensure pupils don't leave Year 3 thinking all shapes are perfectly symmetrical and give them a diet where the polygons come in all shapes and sizes.

Wood or plastic?

In terms of preparing children to draw accurate shapes you must ensure that they are using the isometric or squared paper as carefully as possible, within millimetres of the precise measurement. Isometric paper is useful when starting out and will act as a decent guideline. The peg board activities using elastic or rubber bands can be used as a model and will make pupils consider the properties when creating the shapes. I would highly recommend any measuring is done with a plastic ruler and any line drawing with a wooden ruler; the numbers on a plastic ruler tend to become obscured by pen marks if they are used for anything other than measuring and this would leave them mathematically redundant and obsolete in the classroom.

Once again the necessity to keep pupils aware of the range of orientations shapes may take becomes apparent as pupils are expected to *identify lines of symmetry in 2-D shapes presented in different orientations*. Without experience of seeing shapes in different orientations they will be deskilled and unaware of the need to rotate, explore, transpose, translate, anything needed to try to identify the symmetry lurking within shapes. Hopefully a consistent approach to the curriculum will allow you to build but if not refer to earlier guidance and advice regarding the orientation of shapes. Note the non-statutory guidance – pupils must be able to identify symmetry where the line of symmetry does not dissect the original shape. The breadth of symmetrical knowledge in these few objectives is greater than it appears on the surface.

Measure of turn

As we already know an angle is a measure of turn, they are recorded in degrees, and they can be acute, obtuse and right to those with a very basic or elementary understanding. An acute angle is less than 90 degrees, a right angle 90 degrees exactly and an obtuse angle greater than 90 degrees but less than 180 degrees. The two straight sides are called arms and where they meet is known as the vertex, naturally, so when describing the measurement of an angle with a protractor you need to match up the line at the bottom of the protractor with one of the arms and place the bubble in the middle of the protractor on the vertex. This use of language makes that description infinitesimally more clear than saying put the line on the line and the bubble in the middle. The angle is the amount of turn between each arm and this should be shown to pupils, perhaps even through the use of their own arms. The orientation of the angle is important but not just yet so focus on introducing the basics and providing that oh so necessary foundation for your Year 5 colleagues.

The *identification of right angles, recognising that two right angles make a half-turn, three makes three quarters of a turn and four a complete turn; identifying whether angles are greater than or less than a right angle* seems a lot of information for just one sentence in the statutory guidance and as such should be broken down into smaller pieces.

Pupils have previously explored the concept of turning, both clockwise and anti-clockwise at quarter, half and three quarter trajectories, but the main focus of the learning was on the positional movement and the physical turn made by the person. And it appears this was done on purpose because position and movement does not feature in the Year 3 curriculum. It appears a mere precursor to the pupils' understanding of angles. With this in mind it is here we need to link it to the properties of the shape and the understanding of a right angle as a quarter turn.

Robot rock

You may wish to draw links to computing and make robots or onscreen software follow a range of instructions. There are often programs in which the main character receiving the instruction draws a line which, when manipulated correctly, can create any shape you wish. Such an activity can then transfer into the drawing of shapes following similar instructions from a partner or yourself but the real key is to link this to architectural planning. How can we draw an accurate blue-print if we don't use the correct shapes to represent the rooms?

Once the pupils have grasped the concept of the turn you will be able to open up the possibility of angles being greater than or less than 90 degrees. Non-statutory guidance explains that you should be accurate in your use of language and that the terms acute and obtuse describe angles greater or lesser than a right angle. It is important here to ensure you have described the angles and the parts which come together to create them.

I am surprised to see little change in the content covered by the properties of shapes in Year 5 and I see little difference even between the same point in the old and new curricula. A consideration for another day perhaps as my aim is not to question why but to identify, prevent and address misconceptions taking into account the statutory nature of the requirements outlined. I reiterate that the progression throughout this section of this book is but one and there may be many interpretations. This just happens to be the expected progression at the time of writing and a reasonable progression to begin your journey towards full blown expertise with.

Notice the introduction of reflex angles when measuring, estimating and comparing angles. Identical principles apply to those in Year 4 and as such you should be sure your vocabulary matches up. Be sure to check the mini-glossary for Year 4 and you can be certain to be on the right track. A reflex angle, for posterity, is an angle greater than 180 degrees but less than 360 degrees. There is an expectation that pupils identify angles at 360 degrees, 180 degrees and other multiples of 90 degrees and while this will be useful in solving problems it will not be possible without an understanding of multiples of 9. Ensure the pupils have this knowledge and combine the two.

More difficult, however, is the understanding of the concept of symmetry. While it is beneficial to maintain an accurate approach to the description of symmetrical we must be sure that they not only understand but that they can *complete a simple symmetric figure with respect to a specific line of symmetry*. This, I propose, is a more difficult skill than identifying symmetry alone and there has been very little mention of symmetry up to this point; we must make sure that our children are prepared through a suitable progression rather than rushing through the steps towards an end which makes no sense at all.

The non-statutory guidance suggests you draw lines to the nearest millimetre, something I'd recommend from much earlier and that the conventional markings for parallel lines and right angles are used. I'm not entirely sure why this isn't mentioned in the actual requirement itself but be aware of the need to do so.

With such small additions in content knowledge I feel you will have time to ensure your opportunities are rich in mathematics and that shape is championed as something more than just general knowledge. There should be very little new to teach here so maximise your pupils' time by enhancing the quality of their access to the properties of shape. If you don't you'll be doing them a disservice.

I was surprised to see that the *illustration and naming of parts of circles, including radius, diameter and circumference, knowing that the diameter is twice the radius* remained in Year 6 but it has. I thought the expectation would be moved to Year 5 to make room for further use of this knowledge but it was not to be this time. The relationship between the three aspects of a circle are key and as such they have been defined clearly below:

- *Radius* – a straight line from the centre to the circumference of a circle.
- *Diameter* – a straight line passing from side to side through the centre of a body or figure, especially a circle or sphere.
- *Circumference* – the enclosing boundary around a geometric shape such as a circle.

πr^2

The various formulae associated with circles could potentially be used as a starting point when trying to encourage the usual greater depth of understanding. How the pupils apply them will depend on their confidence and fluency in a number of key areas and should be given full consideration when planning in those challenging activities and opportunities. Not all of them will be appropriate for your pupils but here they are, presented as clearly as I can find possible.

Area

- The area of a circle is equal to Pi multiplied by the radius squared.
- $A = \pi r^2$

Circumference

- The circumference of a circle is equal to Pi multiplied by the diameter.
- $C = 2\pi r$
- The circumference of a circle is equal to two times Pi times the radius.
- $C = 2\pi r$

Radius

- The radius of a circle is equal to the diameter divided by two.
- $r = d/2$ (*But that one is pretty straightforward indeed.*)
- The radius of a circle is equal to the square root of the area divided by Pi.
- $r = \sqrt{(A / \pi)}$
- The radius of a circle is equal to the circumference divided by two times Pi.
- $r = C / 2\pi$

Ensure your pupils are aware of the language that is needed to describe and the understanding will come through application of that very same vocabulary. Where pupils are expected to *recognise angles where they meet at a point, are on a straight line, or are vertically opposite, and find missing angles* the language of angles as outlined before is key but also the application and reasons for application. To prevent misconceptions you must ensure pupils understand the key vocabulary, particularly those parts involved in measurement with a protractor. A wide range of opportunities will ensure pupils access everything in this requirement and the more meaningful they are they more secure they will be. Feel free to try to blow their minds with your knowledge of the theory of infinite sides mentioned at the very beginning of our journey together, though do put down some sheets first.

11 Geometry – position and direction

In my humble opinion, it goes without saying that geometry has always been of mathematical significance to primary practitioners and I am pleased to see its formal introduction in the 2014 National Curriculum. I feel it must be noted at this point that mental geometry is equally, if not more so, important to pupil progress and should be considered in tandem with its more literal counterpart. Mental methods should always be taught in conjunction with written method as you well know and here this particular canon comes into its own. If pupils can select complementary mental operations to those they must record in writing then I truly believe the efficiency of their methods will be multiplied tenfold.

Patterns

When *ordering and arranging combinations of mathematical objects in patterns and sequences* we see the beginnings of algebraic formulation. Patterns in colour and shape are the building blocks of reasoning and mathematical creativity. They have the potential to stretch as far as the mind can conceive and it is the role of the Year 2 teacher to embrace this prospect in our current statutory guidance.

Structure

When considering the lesson structure and content you must begin with the questions you want your pupils to ask. *What is the next term in the sequence?* Term a prefatory statement of what eventually lies in store. *Can I alter the sequence? What happens if … When is … not true … Can I formulate a rule?* Rule, another precursor of things to come.

What appears to be a general identification of patterns can be drawn out into the formation of reasoning and deductive skills pupils will enjoy and capitalise on for the rest of their mathematical careers. There is a plethora of investigative work, differentiated for a range of developmental levels, which can be accessed online and I would encourage you whole-heartedly to do so. Some examples have been provided in Figure 11.1 and they

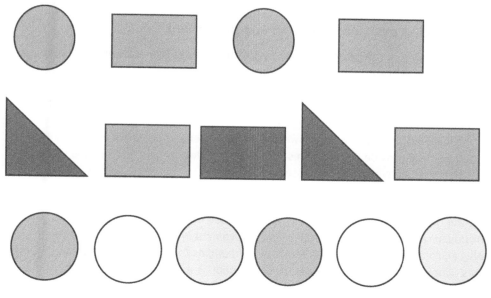

Figure 11.1

can be used as a basis through which to formulate lessons and investigations of your own. What is key is that the diet is rich and the opportunities are recognised as more than a mere ordering of the facts. The facts, however important, come second to mathematical understanding and this needs to be appreciated. Just as shapes are more than mere fact, sequences and patterns are akin to the building blocks of life. They are the Higgs boson of primary mathematics. Respect them, utilise them and, most of all, enjoy them.

Turns

A straightforward explanation is necessary for the use of any language but particularly when *describing position, direction and movement, including whole, half, quarter and three-quarter turns*. Identify this language and use it frequently. It shouldn't just be a case of when the time comes to introduce this topic pupils are taught the language and we move on. Instead this language should become part of their everyday discourse. The familiarity will increase the depth of understanding, the range of cues to draw on when remembering the meaning of the language, and allow pupils to apply fluently much earlier than if it is taught discretely in isolation from its true application. What's that I hear you say? Hoorah, a triumphant return for position and direction? Indeed what was momentarily banished to the wilderness, the veritable back benches of Year 3, has returned stronger than ever before in Year 4 National Curriculum requirements. I can only imagine why this was left out in the previous year group but now that it is back we must consider the raised expectations for our Year 4 children and how to best meet their needs.

Describing position, direction and movement

You may want to consider how it may be possible to make this relevant to the umbrella topic covered, the pupils' lives in general or how you can make the learning concrete before creating an abstract context in which to apply the necessary skills. This may include treasure maps, Roman legions or anything you can think of that will link with the learning that needs to take place.

However, once you have drawn concrete reference points from which to lead I suggest you provide opportunities for pupils to follow or give instructions involving the skills you have so skilfully disseminated.

You will then notice that pupils are expected to *use mathematical vocabulary to describe position, direction and movement, including movement in a straight line and distinguishing between rotation as a turn and in terms of right angles for quarter, half and three-quarter turns (clockwise and anti-clockwise).* This, no doubt, is a veritable mouthful and should, in my opinion, not be treated as one objective. Indeed there are several which can be drawn from it and it is my intention to provide examples of this when making reference to the skills and language necessary to prevent the development of misconceptions.

Initially I would begin by ensuring pupils *learn to use mathematical vocabulary to describe position, direction and movement.* This, of course, will include movement in a straight line but it does not necessarily mean you will cover a comparison between it and rotation. I would suggest an opening session which involved the use of the terms: close, middle, near, around, above, far, in front of, below, inside, beside, halfway, next to, bottom, between, grid, position, front and centre.[1] They really are as simple as they appear to be and should form the basis of a practical lesson where pupils are in those positions, describing the position of others and identifying the relationship between the concept and the written words.

Pupils will already be used to graph work through their statistical analysis of previous years but this will be the first time they will be expected to draw a pair of axes as a quadrant. Often as a child I would hear people talking about going across the corridor and up the stairs but I would recommend you treat the pupils with a bit more respect and explain that we read the coordinates x axis, y axis. It's in alphabetical order which is always handy and you could explain that we read horizontal before vertical but please don't cheapen the value of the concept with corridors and stairs.

Once this understanding is embedded pupils will then be *required to translate left, right, up and down* through the quadrant and *plot specific points and draw sides to complete a given polygon.* They will, it seems, be expected to apply their knowledge from the off so I would go ahead and give it some relevance. What mathematical relevance does this have for my pupils? What real life application is there for my pupils? There are certainly computing links to be made but think of the wider picture and try to find those meaningful links to the lives of our pupils. They will also need to remember the key components to drawing mathematical shapes.

The expectation for position and direction is simple and straightforward in Year 5. Pupils must *identify, describe and represent the position of a shape following a reflection or translation, using the appropriate language, and know that the shape has not changed.* You'll be wondering what the appropriate language is but you need look no further than the guidance. They must know that parallel describes lines which are side by side and have the same distance between them continuously and that axes are fixed reference lines for the measurement of coordinates and, in our case, translating and reflecting shapes.

The four almighty quadrants

As pupils are expected to *describe positions on the full coordinate grid (all four quadrants)* we would hope that they understood negative numbers, scaled divisions on a graph, axes, coordinates and statistical analysis. The reason being that these are the aspects necessary to describe positions on the full coordinate grid. The knowledge of coordinates in one quadrant can be applied to all four if the pupils are aware of the use of negative numbers in three of the four quadrants.

Once this is secure you may then explore the concept of *rotation as a turn and right angles for quarter, half and three-quarter turns (clockwise and anti-clockwise)*. It is easy to include clockwise and anti-clockwise in your everyday descriptive dialogue and I would encourage this as the most effective way for pupils to assimilate the language. *Let's share our ideas, we will move clockwise around the class.* Treasure hunts are the perfect way to introduce the idea of rotation as a turn, and if you insist the pupils only use the terms you want them to in their instructions then you will have covered the geometric requirements in a practical and engaging manner. The notes and guidance suggest this is the perfect time to link the mathematical learning with the development of computing skills. Mathematics often overlaps with scientific and technological learning and it is always worth being aware of the possibilities within your own school setting.

When the links are made and opportunities provided it is important to include accurate description of rotation, turn, right angles, quarter, half and three-quarter turns, as always, to ensure accurate understanding of the inherent concepts and as such a mini-glossary has once again been included. Please refer to this as you plan and include opportunities for discussion, instruction and direction.

Key vocabulary

- *Half turn* - a turn of 180 degrees.
- *Quarter turn* - a turn of 90 degrees.
- *Right angle* - 90 degrees.
- *Rotation* - the action of rotating about an axis or centre.
- *Three-quarter turn* - a turn of 270 degrees.
- *Turn* - the act of moving something in a circular direction around an axis or point.

Pupils must also be able to draw shapes, predict missing coordinates using the properties of shapes and manipulate the quadrants as fluently as possible when *drawing and translating simple shapes on the coordinate plane, and reflecting them in the axes*. Initially I was of the opinion that there isn't really much to say at this point and in reference to this requirement other than to insist that you go back and fill the gaps if your pupils cannot see the concept which in actual fact is rather concrete in comparison with some of the others in the Year 6 curriculum. That was, however, before tracing paper was outlawed by the powers that be and removed from the list of acceptable resources to be used during the end of Key Stage 2 standardised assessments.

Tracing paper

Even though it shouldn't have caused any major issues this slight alteration to the assessment arrangements became a bit of a game changer, largely due to the fact that pupils would need to understand the concepts of translation, rotation and reflection fully without the ability to rely on tracing paper as a crutch which could very often do the work for them come that most important of weeks in early May. That is not to say that every Year 6 pupil used this method and that our nation is awash with grown men and women who can't define the aforementioned terms but if not for this purpose then why else was tracing paper included in the first place?

Same or similar?

In terms of knowledge key to pupil understanding we must consider the congruency of shapes which have been translated, rotated or reflected. As long as size hasn't been altered then they have, for all intents and purposes, the potential to become the translation, reflection or rotation following one or more of those actions. If the shape is resized then they cannot be congruent as this would merely describe a shape with similar properties rather than one which is congruent. The word congruent embodies quite a bit of information and is a prime example of the succinct proficiency of reasoning which can be achieved through accurate use of mathematical language.

Note

1   All referenced on a handy twinkl.co.uk poster.

12 Epilogue

I cannot stress enough how important it is pupils receive a diet of mathematics which is consistent, high in quality, as broad and varied as possible and rooted in real life relevancy. I hope that my explanations and advice have gone some way to helping you provide access to the highest mathematical expectations for your pupils and your peers whether they are currently embodied in the 2014 English National Curriculum or that of a different geographical body. Wherever your career takes you I implore you to remember, if nothing else, that the need for accurate and concise mathematical language is one of the greatest contributors to mathematical understanding.

Combine this with a rich and varied combination of real life application and investigation and you will have a recipe for success. If you want to share your experience, suggest a mathematically rich investigation or seek further advice then you have that opportunity via Twitter, @Kieran_M_Ed. That is not to say that I am the omnipotent and omnipresent oracle, far from it, but I am always happy to share my experience. If nothing else at all remember that what we do has a profound impact on the children in our care, whether positive or negative, and that with great power comes great responsibility. I wasn't dressed as Spiderman, let's see how quickly that already out of date popular culture reference ages, when I said that but you can bet if I can find a mathematical link then the first chance I get I'll be togged in red and blue spandex and hanging from the ceiling. That's how far I'd go and how far I want you to go! So go, and be the best you can be for all our children.

Index